W9-CJQ-441

GREECE AND ROME

Published in 1996 by
Marshall Cavendish Corporation
99 White Plains Road
Tarrytown, NY 10591-9001
U.S.A.

Editor: Henk Dijkstra
Executive Editor: Paulien Retèl
Revision Editor: Frits Naerebout (The Greek City-States, The Peloponnesian War, Greece after the Classical Period,
Alexander the Great, Hellenism, The Greek Legacy), Henk Singor (Ancient Rome, Patricians and Plebeians, From City to State,
Duel for the West, The Roman Revolution)
Art Director: Henk Oostenrijk, Studio 87, Utrecht, The Netherlands
Index Editors: Schuurmans & Jonkers, Leiden, The Netherlands
Preface: Suzanne Heim, Ph.D. Ancient Near East and Classical Art and Archaeology
Translated by: EuroNet Language Services, Inc. New York, NY 10018

The History of the Ancient & Medieval World is a completely revised and updated edition of *The Adventure of Mankind.*
©1996 Marshall Cavendish Corporation, Tarrytown, New York, and HD Communication Consultants BV,
Hilversum, The Netherlands

Library of Congress Cataloging-in-Publication Date

History of the ancient and medieval world / edited by Henk Dijkstra.
p. cm.
Completely rev. and updated ed. of: The Adventure of mankind (second edition 1996).
Contents:—v.5. Greece and Rome.
ISBN 0-7614-0356-6 (v.5).—ISBN 0-7614-0351-5 (lib.bdg.:set)
1. History, Ancient—Juvenile literature. 2. Middle Ages—History—Juvenile literature. I. Dijkstra, Henk. II Title: Adventure of mankind.
D117.H57 1996
930—dc20/95-35715

History of the
Ancient & Medieval World

Volume 5

Greece
and Rome

Marshall Cavendish
New York Toronto Sydney

Greece and Rome

HEKATE

Detail of the altar of Zeus in Pergamon, Turkey, dating from the Hellenistic period

CONTENTS

Preface

The political organization of Greece comprising autonomous city-states served more to foster rivalries than lasting alliances as Greek civilization reached its zenith in the Classical period (fifth century BC). After defeating the common enemy, Persia, the two most powerful city-states, Sparta and Athens, engaged in the bitter Peloponnesian War, while Athens under the leadership of Pericles simultaneously reached great heights culturally.

With the defeat of Athens followed by continued skirmishes among the city-states, a new power was on the rise in the north in Macedonia. By the end of the fourth century BC, Alexander the Great ruled Greece and marched a huge army into the Near East, conquering the expanse of the Persian Empire and beyond and making it his own.

For two centuries (third and second centuries BC) Alexander's successors (the diadochs) ruled this empire causing an intermixing of Greek culture with that of the varied indigenous Near Eastern peoples. Advances in scholarship in the arts and sciences including literature, philosophy, mathematics, and medicine continued in this period and an important learning center was established at Alexandria in Egypt.

While the Greek city-states were developing and colonies were set up in southern Italy in the eighth century BC, most of the Italian Peninsula was inhabited by various tribes including the Latins, Sabines, and Etruscans. The legendary founding of Rome by Romulus and Remus in 753 BC begins the long history of the powerful city and its growth into a city-state and imperial military power.

The development of the government of the Roman Republic is well documented in numerous sources written in Latin which also give a vivid picture of the personalities involved. A class structure of privileged patricians and peasant plebeians formed the basis of the system which had a senate, an assembly, and at first a king who was replaced by consuls. The army was also strictly organized, often having power of its own. Class struggles led to the establishment of written laws designed to protect the rights and property of all men (except slaves).

Tribal rivalries in the Italian Peninsula contributed to the rise of Rome and by the third century BC it had controlled most of the peninsula and turned to deal with the other great Mediterranean power, Carthage, based in North Africa. Long campaigns were waged (the Punic Wars) during much of the third century BC. By 201, Rome had conquered Carthage and its subjects including Sicily and Spain, thus ruling the west.

Warfare continued in the east (Greece, Asia Minor, Syria) and such prolonged campaigns and conquests led to changes and corruption in Roman society. A long line of public officials during the third and second centuries BC attempted to redress the ills by pressing for reforms—a movement which would continue. The second century brought yet more war abroad (Macedonia, Carthage again, Spain, northern German tribes) as well as at home in the first century (the Social War in Italy). All the while, the Roman republican system was tested and threatened by corruption in the senate and the dictatorship of Sulla (82 BC) who continued to favor the aristocracy. It would take a special personality to effect real and lasting change in govenment.

Suzanne Heim, Ph.D.,
Ancient Near East and
Classical Art and Archaeology

Ruins of a temple of the god Apollo at Bassae, as they can still be seen on the Peloponnisos, dating from c. 420 BC

The Greek City-states

A Conflict Arises

Characteristics

By the seventh century BC, Greece was divided into *poleis*, small independent city-states. With the exception of a few larger ones, these often encompassed no more than a little town or village and its surrounding territory. Yet they succeeded in remaining autonomous, each greatly prizing its independence. Mountains separated many of them, adding to their isolation. Their borders, vaguely defined, ran through disputed country inhabited largely by shepherds and woodcutters. Mount Olympus, considered the abode of the gods, at 9,570 feet (2,917 meters) high, dominated the central Pindus Mountains. Below it, on the southeastern plains of the mainland, lay most of the city-states of the mainland. Sparta dominated the large peninsula called the Peloponnisos.

Despite unmistakable similarities in language and religion among them, the cultural differences of the city-states must not be underestimated. Local religious idiosyncrasies abounded; each city-state had its own myths and legends (which frequently portrayed "the others" as the enemy). Each spoke a local dialect and had its own customs. (Athenians, for instance, were shocked and fascinated by the relative freedom that Spartan women enjoyed.)

Open and Closed Societies

Some city-states were relatively closed societies; others were more open. Their internal or external orientation was apparent in their economic life. The city-states were by no means equally active in domestic trade and export; many, like Sparta, were solidly agrar-

A lady takes off her jewels and puts them in a box held for her by a servant. This scene is depicted on the Greek grave monument of Hegeso, dating from the fifth century BC.

ian, self-sufficient in food and dependent on the outside world to only a limited extent. Athens was quite the opposite, opting for large-scale food import and active commerce with the outside world.

The contrast between closed and open societies was evident in the social structure, as well. In some city-states, the inhabitants comprised two groups, citizens with full civil rights and second-class citizens or, as in the case of Sparta, serfs. In other territories,

all the inhabitants (at least the adult males; females were rarely granted rights) enjoyed the same civil rights. Here again, Athens, with its equal rights for all (males), and Sparta constitute examples of the two extremes. Political organization differed from one city-state to the next. Regardless of how citizenship was defined, not all citizens shared equally in the government. Athens was a special case, with its radically comprehensive democracy. Democracy did exist in other city-states, but various forms of *oligarchy* (rule by a few) were much more common. Oligarchies and democracies were wary of each other, fearful that the dissidents among their own people would gain support elsewhere. Over the course of time, political ideology was to play an increasingly significant role in the conflicts between city-states, with Athens and Sparta at the forefront.

Aggression was built into Greek society. The city-states were highly competitive. The paramount way to gain honor and glory—and the spoils, too, of course—was to conquer another city-state. States in danger of falling victim to their neighbor's pursuit of power tried to maintain their independence. Those who had already lost their independence tried to regain it. States in both positions signed treaties with each other as a precaution, rarely hesitating to form alliances even with their traditional common enemy, Persia. Even when city-states were well matched and there was no real question of one subjugating the other, border disputes would continue. Any interstate coalitions that were established for mutual protection tended to be transient in nature. Underlying them was a permanent condition of rivalry that resulted in incessant war. It was this, above all else, that hindered any real unity among the city-states.

Background of City-state Conflict

The Greek city-states, first conquered by Croesus, king of Lydia, in Asia Minor, were made part of the Persian Empire in 546 BC when Croesus himself was ousted by Cyrus the Great, king of Persia. Only the island of Samos was able to resist. In 499 BC Ionia rebelled, aided by Athens and Eretria, initiating the Persian Wars. Six years later, King Darius I of Persia reasserted his control over Ionia, sacking its major city, Miletus. In 492 BC, he sent his son-in-law Mardonius with an enormous fleet against the remaining rebel Greeks. The ships were wrecked off Mount Athos. When the king sent messengers out to demand surrender, most of the Greek city-states complied. Sparta and Athens refused, killing the Persian messengers, heralding their dominance in the Greek

Scene from the legend of Jason and Medea, as represented on a *sarcophagus* (stone coffin) relief

world. The Athenian army alone defeated a Persian force three times its size on the plains of Marathon near Athens in 490 BC. The powerful Spartan army, busy with a religious festival, did not come to Athens's assistance. A decade later, the Spartans found their army less important than the Athenian navy. The decisive battle of the Persian War was a naval engagement off Salamis, an island in the Gulf of Aegina (now called the Saronic Gulf) near Athens. Some 400 Greek ships, under the command of the Athenian Themistocles, defeated 1,200 Persian vessels.

The Delian League

The triumphant Athens established the Delian League in 478 BC, a voluntary alliance to rid the city-states and Greek islands of the remaining Persians. As it achieved a series of victories under the Athenian general Cimon between 476 and 466 BC, Athens increasingly took over. The league soon became more of an Athenian empire than a confederation. Athens even asked for payment of tribute from its "allies." When the island of Naxos refused and tried to withdraw from the alliance, Athens destroyed its fortifications.

Bust of Thucydides, the most famous historian of ancient Athens. He lived between c. 460 and 400 BC.

585

Statue of Euripides, an Athenian playwright who lived in the fifth century BC. During his life he was not so very popular, but this has changed in the course of time. Of the nineteen plays that have survived and are still staged today, his *Medea* and *Bacchai* are the best known. The plays are listed behind the statue.

Sparta and Athens: The Roots of Conflict

In 460 BC, the great statesman Pericles was made both the leader of the popular party and the head of the state. He led Athens to its greatest political and cultural achievements but (from the Spartan viewpoint) his pretension in seeing Athens as the capital of all of Greece was unacceptable. Pericles used the massive limestone hill called the Acropolis as a showplace for some of the greatest architecture the world had ever seen. He had the structure called the Propylaea built as the entrance to it. He erected the Parthenon, a Doric temple to Athena, the goddess of wisdom and patron deity of Athens. To balance it politically, he had the Ionian temple, the Erechtheum, constructed. As these and other notable buildings rose, Sparta, also a victor and a leader in the Persian Wars, watched with disappointment.

Pericles encouraged the development of Greek art and drama, as well. Aeschylus, Euripides, and Sophocles wrote and presented their tragedies. Aristophanes penned his comedies. Thucydides and the Ionian Herodotus wrote the first histories of Greece. Socrates and Plato taught their respective philosophies. Athens became the undisputed artistic and intellectual center of Greece, but Sparta found it intolerable to have to accept the political leadership of its former rival.

It retreated into self-elected isolation on the Peloponnisos to strengthen its own power base. The two city-states ended up in opposition to each other: the open Athens, an expansive naval power, progressive and democratic, and the closed Sparta, an isolated land power, conservative and oligarchic. Over the course of the fifth century, the contrasts became sharper. Athens became increasingly self-confident, more aggressive in its foreign affairs as it broadened its domestic democracy. The militaristic Sparta experienced (by choice) only stagnation. It was leery of an Athens that, from Sparta's perspective, stood for everything that Sparta opposed.

The Peloponnesian War (431–404 BC)

From 460 BC, when Pericles took over the leadership of Athens, to 445 BC, there were only occasional skirmishes between Athens and Sparta or Sparta's allies. This period ended when the parties signed a peace agreement that was supposed to last thirty years. In fact, the armistice lasted only until 431, when full-scale war finally broke out between Sparta and Athens. From 431 to 421 BC, the war was fought with terrible tenacity. Then an armistice (the Peace of Nicias) was declared. The state of peace was sustained only to 418, when fighting resumed. The war continued unabated until 404, when the Spartans dealt the final blow to the Athenians. They destroyed the splendid Athenian fleet, tore down Athens's city walls, and occupied the city. It was this Peloponnesian War that the Greeks spoke of as the "Great War," not the war against the Persians. In contrast to the war against the Persians, which ultimately played itself out in a few major battles, it lasted more than

thirty years. Almost all the Greek city-states took part through alliances with one party or the other. These alliances with Sparta and Athens shifted over the protracted period of conflict. At several points, Dorian states like Megara were allied with Athens. In general, however, Athens's allies were Ionians and Sparta's were Dorians, in line with the ancient rivalry between the Dorians and the Ionians.

Thucydides (c. 460–c. 400 BC)

The *History of the Peloponnesian War* was written by one of its contemporaries, the

A *krater*, a vessel in which wine and water were mixed (the ancient Greeks always diluted their wine with water). It is decorated with a scene from one of Euripides's tragedies, in which the hero Heracles goes insane and kills his wife and children.

Athenian historian Thucydides, a general, who was personally involved in the war's operations. He is said to be the first historian to write "history" in the modern sense of the word. He attempted to give an objective account of the facts known to him, as well as an explanation for the relationship between the events. He had clearly divested himself of older, traditional ways of thinking, making no attempt to explain what was happening in terms of the meddling of the gods in

Fragment of the marble frieze situated on the southern side of the Parthenon, depicting a god and goddess

the affairs of humans, which was the explanation given by the first Greek historian, Herodotus.

Thucydides's view was that historical events were the consequence of both the circumstances of the time and the characters of the leading personalities involved. He compared Sparta to Athens in the following manner: "If the city of Sparta were to be depopulated so that only the temples and public buildings remained, then I believe that in due course someone visiting the city would not be able to believe that Sparta had been as powerful a state as it currently is. But if the city of Athens were to have the same fate, a person visiting her later would think that she had been even greater and more powerful

than she actually is today—just from seeing the ruins and the enormous space they occupy." Thucydides's comparison had a touch of the prophetic, for anyone traveling to Sparta today will find a quite insignificant rural town without many monuments (and what is to be seen is often relatively recent historically). Athens, on the other hand, still boasts numerous ruins of temples, theaters, marketplaces, and other monuments, despite its eventful history. The city once shrank to a small village, only to reestablish itself as a modern city with over a million inhabitants.

Battle Tactics

In all the years of the war, the tactics of the warring parties never really altered significantly. Athens remained faithful to the imperialistic policy of Pericles, its leader, even after his death in 429 from the plague, concentrating its attention on the fleet they depended on to protect the state's overseas connections. The armies of Sparta, Thebes, and Corinth entered Attica territory, the country villages in the federation led by Athens, and devastated the surrounding country. Recognizing that any land defense against Sparta was impossible, the Athenians retreated inside the walls that enclosed the city.

Fortifications called the "Long Walls" also protected a strip of land that linked the city to the port of Piraeus. Without this access to the sea, Athens would have been unable to get provisions to feed the civilian inhabitants and the military, and would have been starved into submission. The guarded route allowed the city to continue the war, mounting expeditions from Piraeus against the coasts of Sparta.

The war tactics of Sparta, predominantly a land power, were entirely different. Every year Spartan soldiers attacked Attica when its grain was ripe for harvest. They laid waste the crops and forced the peasantry to seek refuge inside the Long Walls and the city walls. Eventually they stopped their seasonal retreat to their distant stronghold and stayed permanently on the plains of Attica. This had a twofold effect: Athens was made even more dependent on the import of foreign grain, while the population that consumed that grain increased due to the influx of refugees from the outlying regions. The large concentration of people within the walls fostered the sort of plague that killed Pericles. Sparta would ultimately force the weakened Athens to its knees.

In a scene that was popular in Attic art during the fifth century BC, a soldier says good-bye to his grieving family with a ritual parting drink. The red-figured vase dates from around 430 BC.

The Peloponnesian War

The Greek City-states Side with Athens or Sparta

The Peloponnesian War began in 431 BC, when the long-standing competition between Athens and Sparta could no longer be contained. Thucydides, although the son of an aristocratic Athenian, determined to document it in as unbiased fashion as possible. He wrote his *History of the Peloponnesian War* from somewhat limited firsthand experience. He was made one of the generals of the Athenian fleet in 424 BC and ordered to sea to assist the city of Amphipolis, under Spartan siege. By the time he arrived, the city had already been taken. He was banished from Athens (a standard punishment) and lived twenty years abroad until recalled in 404 BC. His book examines three phases of the Peloponnesian War, although his history ends in 411 BC. (The war went on until 404 BC.) He details the conflict between Athens and Sparta, ended by the Peace of Nicias, the Athenian expedition to Sicily, and the renewal of the war.

Athens and Sparta Fight for Supremacy (431–421 BC)

During the Peloponnesian War, the nature of warfare itself changed. Military operations were massive in scale and far more intensive. Foot soldiers (*hoplites*) were deployed, but new lighter-armed troops and cavalry were also used. The troops were increasingly mercenaries. Instead of a "fighting season" with battles fought on battlefields, guerrilla tactics were adopted and used year-round. Fighting became increasingly savage. The populations of entire cities were enslaved or put to the sword. In the decades preceding the outbreak of war, there had been skirmishes between Athens and Sparta (with no assistance from Sparta's Dorian allies). Athens had risen to prosperity and predominance in Greece and was widely resented by the city-states allied in the Delian League. Sparta had dominated its own allies, the Peloponnesian League, since about 550 BC. It moved to bring down Athens in 431 BC, beginning three decades of war. The immediate cause of war was the fact that Athens assisted the island of Corcyra (Corfu) in a dispute between Corcyra and Corinth, an ally of Sparta. Corcyra had long been a colony of Corinth and was, therefore, part of the Dorian sphere of influence. This state had, in turn, founded its own colony by the name of Epidamnus. When a vehement dispute erupted between Epidamnus and Corcyra, the inhabitants of Epidamnus called on Corinth for help. This was a traditional procedure, as Corinth was the *metropolis* (mother city) of both colonies. Corcyra, however, now feeling threatened by Corinth,

Greek grave relief depicting a soldier who takes leave of his wife. The top part is unfortunately lost, so that their faces can no longer be seen.

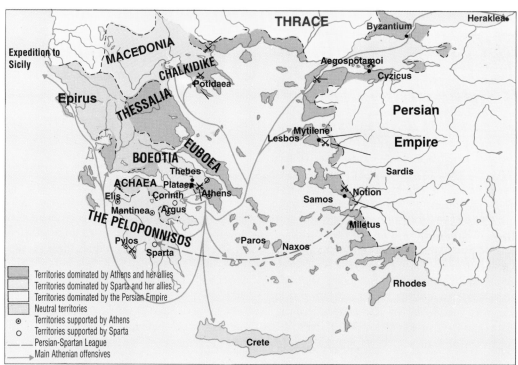

This map depicts the course of the Peloponnesian War

Territories dominated by Athens and her allies
Territories dominated by Sparta and her allies
Territories dominated by the Persian Empire
Neutral territories
⊙ Territories supported by Athens
○ Territories supported by Sparta
—— Persian-Spartan League
→ Main Athenian offensives

decided to join the opposing and powerful Athens-run Delian League. Athens was happy to see the island join the coalition, as Corcyra maintained a fleet of 120 war vessels. United with Athens's own fleet, it was capable of dominating all of Greece.

According to Thucydides, Archidamus, king of Sparta, made a final attempt to reason with the allies and avoid a direct confrontation. As commander in chief of the allied armies, he urged the members of the Peloponnesian Alliance to review the situation before acting.

Archidamus was right, although his advice went unheeded. In 431 the money lay in the Athenian treasury. As the war began, Pericles counted a total of 6,000 *talents* (unit or weight of money) in his reserves. Regardless, the Spartan army struck forcefully, occupying Attica, destroying the harvest, and cutting down the olive trees and grapevines. Such raids became a regular pattern as the Spartans invaded Attica five times. The war expanded, embroiling not only the allies, but several neutral states that chose sides. Proponents of democracy everywhere demanded a treaty with Athens, while advocates of traditional government wanted an alliance with Sparta. The disgruntled colonies jumped at the opportunity to free themselves from the oppressive shackles of Athens.

Yet, despite the calamities Athens suffered during the latter half of the fifth century BC, it continued to experience unprecedented cultural growth. Amid the hardship of war, Athens remained the spiritual center of Greece and the place where science and the arts attained their greatest heights. During the war, Socrates walked the streets of Athens, the Sophists proclaimed their ideas, and Thucydides wrote his major work on the war as it unfolded. The prestigious building projects initiated by Pericles continued unabated. The Parthenon and its sculptures, the beautiful temple of Athena Nike and the Erechtheum with its famous row of caryatids were completed on the Acropolis. This period spawned a great many sculptors, artists, poets, and philosophers. Dramatists (Euripides, Aeschylus, Sophocles, and Aristophanes) wrote tragedies, comedies, and satyr plays, performed to universal acclaim.

Plague in Athens
In 430 an epidemic broke out in the city of Athens, bursting with refugees from the

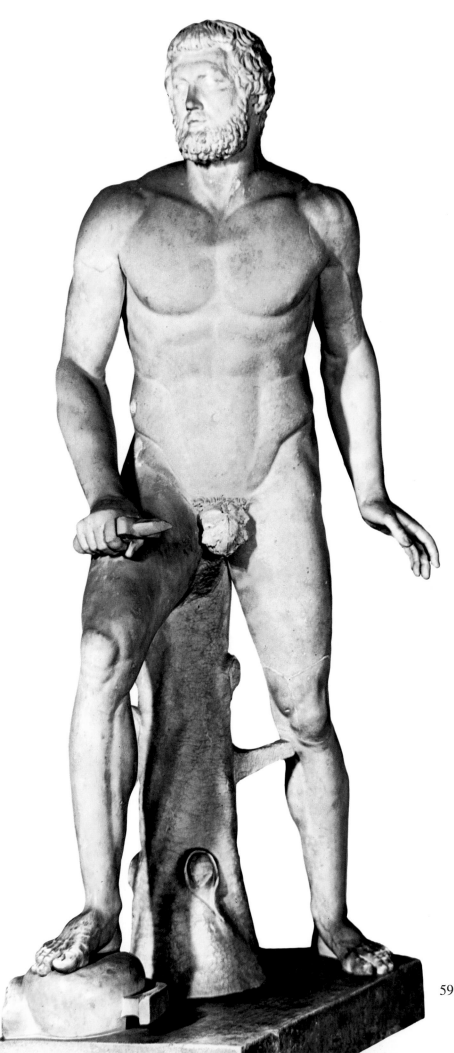

Statue of Alcibiades, Pericles's nephew, who was elected as a general by the people of Athens in 422 BC

Marble head of a mule,
found in Attica, dating from
c. 420–410 BC

Spartan invasions. Thucydides describes this epidemic and all its symptoms, noting that it claimed more victims than all Sparta's campaigns combined. Despite his precise medical description of its symptoms, there is no consensus as to the exact disease which so terrified and ravaged the populace of Athens, but it may have been a plague. He wrote: "I want to discuss this illness so that able physicians may determine whence this evil came and which causes may have produced such a calamity. If this illness returns, everyone shall be warned and take measures. I speak of this epidemic as someone who knows it intimately, for I also was affected and I saw many fall ill and die. That year had been extraordinarily healthy and free of all other disease. But if someone sustained a wound or became ill, it immediately turned into this pestilence. The healthy were suddenly afflicted, without there being an evident rea-

son for their illness. First they would feel a severe headache and their eyes turned red; their throat became inflamed and their breathing labored. Hoarseness, pain in the chest, and mucous cough were followed by painful contractions and convulsions lasting longer with some than with others. The skin swelled up and turned red and was covered with small blisters of pus. Some died after seven or nine days as a result of a burning pain in their intestines. Those still living after this time were struck with stomach pains. After severe diarrhea and cramps, most succumbed from total exhaustion. Most

White painted ⟩
vase depicting Hypnos, the
god of sleep, and
Thanatos, the god of death,
who are laying a dead soldier
to rest, from 450 BC

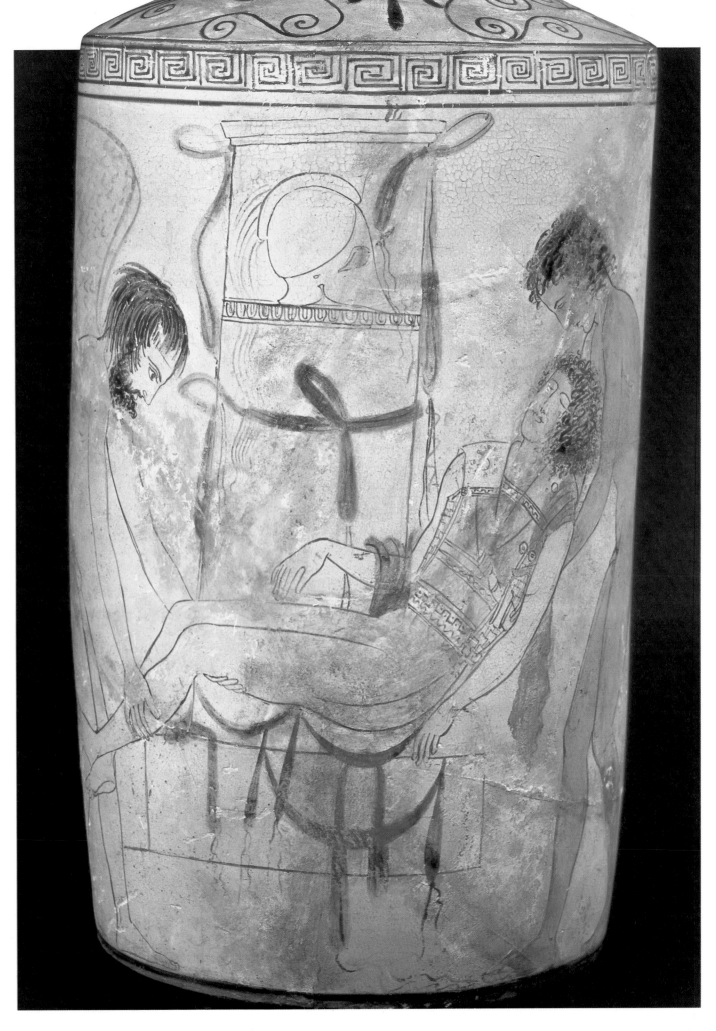

One side of a *trireme*, a Greek man-of-war, with three rows of oarsmen. This marble relief was found on the Acropolis and dates from c. 400 BC.

of the time, the contagion appeared first on the head and subsequently spread over the entire body. Some were blinded or paralyzed; others went mad and did not recognize friends or relatives. Although there were many unburied corpses lying out in the open, the vultures and other scavengers did not come near them, and when they did eat the diseased human flesh, they also died."

The psychological impact of the sudden mass death was as serious as the physical consequences of the epidemic. Thucydides again explains it best: "The have-nots who received an inheritance from rich relatives thought only of publicly showing off their own entertainment. Lest they be afflicted soon themselves, they wanted to enjoy their sudden wealth to the utmost. No one wanted to concern himself with good deeds or long-term commitments because one dared not hope to bring these matters to a good end. All that is pleasant and agreeable to man, the Athenians elevated to virtue and decency. Neither the gods nor commandments were feared, because one believed that it did not matter whether one lived a good or a bad life. Worshiping the gods did not seem to make a difference, because did not both the good

and the bad die equally? And as for the human laws, they believed that they would not live long enough to be prosecuted and punished by the judiciary."

Cleon, Nicias, and Alcibiades Succeed to Power in Athens

When Pericles himself fell victim to the epidemic in 429, power was transferred to Cleon, Nicias, and Alcibiades. These men were probably inadequately equipped to steer Athens through the difficult war. It was difficult to say whether Athens would have fared better with other leaders. Cleon was the major representative of the prowar party, demanding the utmost efforts from both Athenians and allies to continue the war. Although as a general he initially was credited with a few military victories, he did not prove himself the best successor to Pericles. In 422 he was killed in the same battle that saw the death of the important Spartan general Brasidas.

The deaths of Cleon and Brasidas, both of whom had been proponents of continuing the war, cleared the stage for peace negotiations. Nicias (d. 413 BC), another general who had triumphed on the battlefield but was a proponent of peace, managed to reach an agreement with Sparta and the Peloponnesian Alliance in 421 BC. It was called the "Peace of Nicias."

Peace of Nicias

Although Nicias was a righteous man, according to Thucydides, he was also indecisive and dependent. He soon had to relinquish his authority to Alcibiades (c. 450–404 BC), a young, ambitious nobleman. Alcibiades had lost his father at a young age and had been reared by his uncle, Pericles. Apparently Alcibiades had a jovial and charming personality; available sources mention his great popularity. They also describe his appetite for power and his sexuality and other excesses. A dedicated Sophist, he unhesitatingly put their teachings into practice. (The Sophists were a group of philosopher-teachers noted for their skill in making clever but specious arguments.) Alcibiades made politics and law subordinate to his own desires, liberated by his rearing by Pericles and his friendship with Socrates.

In 420, when he was about thirty years old, Alcibiades was called on by the Athenian people to act as *stratēgos* (chief military commander). It was a poor decision because at that very moment Nicias was cautiously trying to end the war that had dragged on for ten miserable years. The fickle Alcibiades, who had gone from endorsing Cleon to supporting Sparta and back again, suddenly saw a way to silence Sparta for

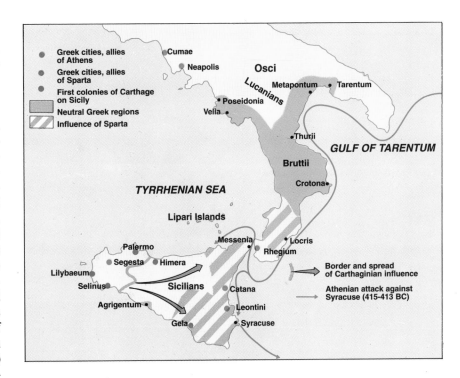

good. He played on the dissatisfaction of some members of the Peloponnesian Alliance with the conditions set forth in the Peace of Nicias. These city-states had rebelled, threatening to weaken or dissolve the alliance. This enhanced Athens's chances for final victory and Alcibiades's desire to return to battle. The war was resumed in 418.

The first conflict ended in miserable defeat for Athens, but this did not end Alcibiades's role. He revived the policies of Pericles, who had aspired to found an empire in the west with Thurii, in southern Italy, as

The course of the Peloponnesian War in the western Greek colonies (southern Italy and Sicily)

Bronze votive lamp shaped as a man-of-war (both sides shown). It was found in the Erechtheum on the Acropolis in Athens and dates from the end of the fifth century BC, the time of the Peloponnesian War.

its center. The Athenian fleet already controlled the Aegean Sea, the Hellespont, and the Bosporus. If Athens could only expand its dominion to the western basin of the Mediterranean, argued Alcibiades, Sparta would be locked up for good on the Peloponnisos, reduced to a subordinate position. His reasoning masked a number of major risks. The plan was not entirely misguided, but its timing was ill-chosen. The impetuous Alcibiades was incapable of carrying it out. He underestimated the Carthaginians who dominated the northern coast of Africa at that time, comparing them to the Phoenicians who obediently followed Persian orders. Carthage, however, was a confident, expanding trading nation, not afraid to face the Athenians. Its presence made full control of the western Mediterranean unlikely, if not impossible.

The Athenian Campaign in Sicily (415–413 BC)

The primary goal of Alcibiades's plan was to gain control of Sicily, which he considered a bridgehead to southern Italy and Africa. A large number of Athenians enthusiastically supported his ambitions, but several cautious men, including Nicias and Socrates, opposed the entire enterprise. The decision was made when a delegation visited from Sicily, consisting of representatives of several cities threatened by the powerful Dorian city of Syracuse, which dominated the island. The Sicilian cities promised Athens their full support in the event of hostilities. The Sophist Gorgias, one of the most eloquent men of his time, accompanied the mission. His arguments were persuasive. Alcibiades's plan encountered little further resistance from the Athenian people's assembly. Nicias, Lamachus, and Alcibiades himself were appointed as leaders of the military expedition to Sicily. A large fleet was outfitted, taking on more than 5,000 heavily armed hoplites in addition to thousands of slingers and other support troops.

Only a handful of men in this proud army would see Athens again, but there was little concern as it set out. Thucydides describes the departure of the fleet in 415 BC as follows: "After the crew had embarked and the sails were hoisted, silence was ordered and the gods were called to aid them. Then the

A coin (a silver tetradrachme) from Syracuse (made in c. 410 BC) showing the goddess Arethusa. It bears the signature of Kimon, one of the best diecutters ever, and dates to 410 BC.

commanders and soldiers and sailors poured libations from gold and silver drinking vessels. On shore those staying behind did the same for their friends and relatives. After singing a hymn and making the offerings, the fleet sailed for Corcyra, where the ships of the Sicilian allies gathered."

From the moment this mighty fleet reached Sicily, everything went wrong. None of the island's Greek colonies was actually willing to participate in the expedition against Syracuse. None wanted to assume the costly provisioning of the Athenian troops, forcing them to look outside the walls where makeshift markets sold supplies at great cost. The cities of Tarentum and Locris even refused to supply fresh water. In spite of such setbacks, Alcibiades succeeded in seizing Catana in a relatively short time, making extensive use of cunning and bribery. Nevertheless, it was an important victory. Catana lay between Syracuse and Messina and could be used to command the strait between Sicily and southern Italy. This maneuver would isolate Syracuse and enable the Athenians to look for allies among the discontented cities on the other side of the strait.

Before Alcibiades had time to put his sly tactics into practice, the court of Athens recalled him in connection with an act of sacrilege. The accusation has come to us as follows: "I, Thessalus, son of Cimon, accuse Alcibiades, son of Clenias, of having mocked the goddesses of Eleusis and having ridiculed their mysteries. Did Alcibiades not walk around in the vestments of the high priest while his friends wore those of the recent initiates?" Alcibiades obediently set out on the return voyage to Athens, but never arrived. He fled instead to Sparta where he became counselor to the enemies of his native city. He was evidently not very confident of the outcome of a trial on his religious views and preferred to commit treason rather than expose himself to the wrath of the Athenians.

In the meantime, the Athenian troops stayed behind under the command of the hesitant Nicias, who had been opposed to the expedition from the start. The siege of Syracuse was a fiasco and cost Athens its fleet and its reputation. Syracuse was an impregnable fortress and could not be cut off. Led by a Spartan general, its inhabitants succeeded in driving the Athenians to the point where Nicias was forced to send a desperate message home for more troops. Athens landed a second army and a second support fleet. Neither was able to salvage the fatal expedition. When Nicias finally decided to abandon the siege of Syracuse and

withdraw in September 413 BC, the retreat degenerated to debacle. Both officers and men were taken prisoner. The leaders, including Nicias, were summarily executed. The soldiers were either made forced laborers in the mines of Syracuse, where they died slow deaths, or were sold as slaves, their foreheads branded with the mark of the city. The people of Syracuse minted beautiful

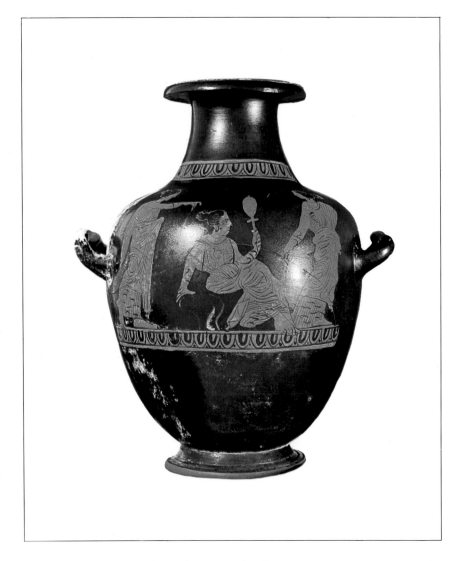

commemorative coins from the proceeds of the Athenian loot.

Renewed War Between Athens and Sparta: 413–404 BC

Alcibiades had done well for himself. Feeling insecure in Sparta, however, he fled to Asia Minor and settled in the court of a *satrap* (governor for the Persian king). From there, he tried to persuade the Persians to conclude an alliance with Athens against Sparta. The resultant powers, he reasoned, could then divide the Mediterranean in separate spheres of influence. This plan failed, driving the distrustful Persians into the arms of Sparta instead of Athens. Alcibiades resumed the battle on the side of Athens, but

Red-figured vase of a woman having her hair styled, from Sicily, fifth century BC

597

despite a few early victories, he was unable to regain a position of trust. Toward the war's end he fled once again, this time to the Persians, who killed him.

Athens Defeated: 404 BC

Athens's fate paralleled that of Alcibiades. He had been able to stretch out his political career until, in effect, it destroyed him. Similarly, Athens was able to hold out against Sparta for another ten years. However, once Persia supported Sparta financially and assisted in building a fleet, Athens's death warrant was signed. Athens had always based its strategy on dominance at sea. When its maritime control was lost in 404 BC, the beleaguered and isolated Athens was forced to surrender. The Delian League was dissolved, the Athenian fleet destroyed, and the walls of Athens razed. Democracy was abolished, replaced by the oligarchy of the "Thirty Tyrants" in 404 and 403 BC.

Sparta had become supreme ruler of all in Greece (404–371 BC), while the Persian Empire, traditional enemy of both Athens and Sparta, looked on benignly. The situation was very much to Persia's advantage. The city-states had exhausted themselves and each other with decades of constant battle. Thebes appeared on the scene as a third great city-state. Battle-weary Athens and Sparta could offer little resistance to a rapidly rising military power to the north of Greece, the Macedonians.

Flourishing Culture in Wartime: Aristophanes and Euripides

Apparently the atmosphere of war had no detrimental effect on the development of the arts, including drama, in Athens. While the city was under siege, Attica in flames, and the Athenian fleet threatened with destruction, Aristophanes (c. 445–385) wrote his biting satirical comedies and Euripides composed the verses of his beautiful tragedies for the contests staged annually in the theater of Dionysus in Athens.

Aristophanes expressed his political and social commentary in fiery comedies that enjoyed great popularity. He did not hide his abhorrence of everything Spartan, though he also criticized Athens's democracy. Aristophanes was often called a conservative because he mocked the democratic leaders.

Red-figured lidded vessel decorated with women's heads, from the fourth century BC

The assessment is incorrect; he satirized everything and everybody. As a comedy writer, his goals were to entertain his audience and to win the annual prize in Athens. Political satire on current events, even ridicule of the government that sponsored the festival of Dionysus, was the way to success.

Aristophanes's plays about war describe the events of the time: firewood is always scarce and olive oil is expensive, while traitors, defectors, defeatists, and war profiteers are numerous. In the *Acharnians* he makes a plea for peace after five years of war, with a peasant concluding his own peace with the Spartans. In the *Knights*, he attacks Cleon, the radical democrat, who is portrayed as a bold slave only outdone by an even fresher sausage-seller. In the *Clouds*, Aristophanes attacks the Sophists and Socrates. In all of the eleven plays that have survived, Aristophanes mocks whatever he disliked in Athenian society and politics.

The Peloponnesian War also left its imprint on the development of tragedy. Twelve years younger than Sophocles (497–406 BC), Euripides (c. 485–406) was a student of Sophism and a personal friend of Socrates. In his comedies, Aristophanes derided Euripides as much as he did Socrates. Euripides was never as popular as Aeschylus (525–456) or Sophocles during his lifetime. His first tri-umph during the festival of Dionysus came only in 441, fourteen years after he began to compete. But as early as the fourth century BC, his work, of which eighteen tragedies, one satyr play, and several loose fragments remain, became quite popular. *Alcestis*, *Medea*, *Andromache*, *Electra*, *Iphigenia in Tauris*, *Orestes*, and the *Bacchae* are among Euripides's most famous plays.

Unlike Sophocles, who tends to idealize his personages, Euripides portrays people as they are, good or bad, subject to passion and magnanimity. Traditional views are frequently the object of Euripides's biting sarcasm, used to such effect that his tragedies almost qualify as comedies. At times he appears the precursor of what is termed the New Comedy of the fourth century BC rather than the last of the great tragedians.

Because of his unadorned language, his fine sense of stage effects, and his capacity to create high tension, Euripides is undoubtedly the most modern of the three major tragedians of the fifth century BC. Today his plays are among those most often performed from the classical repertoire. The Athenians received his commentaries and innovative approach with the same acceptance they showed for the sarcasm of Aristophanes and for the Sophists, but Euripides was not well liked for his denouncing of tradition.

Three tall Attic terra-cotta stands that were used for burning incense, dating from the fifth century

600

An Athenian decree of honor from 373 BC, the year in which one Asteios became *archon* (chief magistrate). His name is mentioned in the top line.

Greece after the Classical Period

Athenian Decline and the Arrival of the Macedonians

At the end of the Peloponnesian War in 404 BC, the Spartan general Lysander proposed peace to the defeated Athens on rather favorable terms. Sparta proposed that Athens be ruled by an *oligarchy*, a government by a few men. The Athenians accepted, thus ensuring that Athens and its allies would remain autonomous and their cities intact. Sparta did, however, demolish the walls of Athens, once crucial to its defense. Sparta also insisted that the Delian League be dissolved. The cities and states of the league were permitted to retain their autonomy, on the condition they replace their democratic

601

Bust of the Attic orator Lysias. This statue is a Roman copy of a Greek portrait dating from the early fourth century BC.

A so-called little bear from the sanctuary of Artemis in Brauron, made in the second half of the fourth century BC. *Little bears* was the name for girls who were initiated in this sanctuary. On that occasion, they offered a little statue of themselves to the goddess.

governments, if any, with oligarchic administrations. Thirty men called oligarchs were appointed to govern Athens and permitted to rule with absolute power for ten months. They were known as the "Thirty Tyrants."

The Thirty Tyrants

The thirty oligarchs could dispose of Athenian citizens' lives and property, protected by a Spartan governor and a small garrison. Spartan-oriented opponents of democracy, the oligarchs tried to settle accounts with their democratic former enemies as soon as possible. The philosopher Theophrastus of Lésvos, one of Aristotle's disciples, described the typical oligarch in his work *Characters* (fourth century BC) as follows: "The oligarch is a man, who while discussing the order of a procession, states the opinion that the leading man must have absolute power; when the people suggest ten leaders, he replies that one leader is sufficient, provided he is a real man. The oligarch only knows one verse of Homer: 'No good shall come of a government by many; one man only must issue the orders.' Oligarchs always say things like: 'We must keep this between us and not discuss it with the crowd, with the market people.'"

Rebellion: 403 BC

The rule of the Thirty Tyrants was so unbearable after one year that the Athenians rebelled in 403 BC. Led by an Athenian named Thrasybulus, they ousted the Spartan garrison that protected the tyrants and reinstated democracy in the city. Throughout the Greek world, other cities revolted against the hegemony of Sparta.

The Orators

The restored democracy heralded a period when great orators controlled the popular assemblies. They were often litigators and legal experts who defended their clients or were called upon to arrange plea bargains for offenses. To influence public opinion, they frequently made use of private matters, citing personal lapses as examples of character and elaborating on them in public. This was particularly the case when criminal charges involved matters of state, such as high treason, fraud, or the incompetence of public officials. Since, in theory, anyone accused in Athens had to argue his own defense, many orators restricted their activities to writing texts for their charged clients to read publicly. It was frequently the case that the orators themselves were the accused in legal proceedings.

Orators who wrote texts for others were called "logographers" or "storywriters."

An Athenian grave
relief made in the middle
of the fourth century BC.
The inscription on
the grave reads as follows:
"Here rests Polyxenos,
who leaves his
young wife, as well
as his father and mother
who gave him his life,
in mourning." In this case,
the relief does not
show the deceased, but
the mourning
relatives.

A 10-foot-
(3-meter-) high statue
of the ruler from
the grave monument of
Mausolos (which is called
the Mausoleum for
that reason), who was a
satrap (provincial
governor of Persia) in
Caria. It was built
in Halicarnassus in the
second half of the
fourth century BC and
became known as
one of the Seven Wonders
of the ancient world.

Even though they themselves did not speak during the legal sessions (they were not allowed to do so if they were not citizens of Athens), several logographers are counted among Attica's best-known orators. Two of the most famous litigators, Isaius and Lysias, were both *metoikes*, or foreigners residing in Athens in the late fifth century BC. Texts by the major logographers excelled because of their splendid use of the Greek language: simple, clear, and elegant. Although they were never as influential as the real orators who made their own speeches, they enjoyed great respect. Nevertheless, men like Demosthenes (c. 384–322 BC) and Isocrates also practiced the profession of logographer out of financial need. Some of the orators, especially the Sophists, acquired a dubious reputation because they were not concerned with the moral aspects of a case.

Lysias of Syracuse

The case of Lysias (c. 459–380 BC) versus Eratosthenes provides excellent illustration of the position of orators in Athenian society. Lysias was a native of the city of Syracuse in Sicily. His father, a manufacturer of armor and shields, had acquired such fame that Pericles invited him to settle in Athens. The arms manufacturer and his two sons (Lysias was the younger) were interested in philosophy and literature. After their father's death, Lysias and his older brother moved to Thurii, Pericles's colony in southern Italy, founded only three years earlier. There, Lysias learned the art of eloquence and persuasion from a famous orator of Syracuse. After the failure of the Athenian campaign in Sicily in 412 BC, the brothers returned to Athens where they earned a fortune with their weapons sales until the end of the Peloponnesian War.

Following Athens's defeat and the installation of the Thirty Tyrants, everyone not pro-Sparta was considered suspect and prosecuted by the rulers. The new government established a reactionary reign of terror, sending scores of people into exile or condemning them to death. Lysias managed to escape and avoided the fate of his brother, who was put to death and his property confiscated. Lysias went into hiding and was one of the conspirators instrumental in unleashing the civil war that restored democracy to Athens. He expended his fortune on the revolutionary cause. When the civil war succeeded in restoring democracy, he was forced to earn a living as a logographer. In his first major trial, he accused his brother's murderers, representing himself in the case. Although as a proponent of democracy he had no civil rights, he was treated as an

Bust of Demosthenes, a famous orator. The head is a Roman copy of an original that was made by the sculptor Polyeuktos in the beginning of the third century BC. The rest of the bust was added at a later date.

The so-called Artemis of Gabii, made between 350 and 330 BC. The goddess is putting on a cloak that she has received as an offering.

equal. Due to the trial's political background, the case attracted a large audience. In effect, the rule of oligarchy was being judged.

Lysias said: "It is a simple matter, Athenians, to begin this charge, but it will be extremely difficult to conclude this charge without forgetting any of the crimes. For the crimes committed by Eratosthenes [one of the oligarchs] are not only severe but also numerous. It is impossible to name them all, let alone describe them, within the time the law has allotted me. Moreover, it is customary during other proceedings for you to ask the public prosecutor what the accused has done. But in this case, you had better ask the accused what terrible thing the motherland has done to him to cause such behavior on his part toward his fellow citizens and his father's city. I do not say this because I want to hide that I have suffered personally because of the accused's actions. But every good citizen feels affected by the calamities committed against his country. I feel a sadness for both reasons and I am of the opinion that I justly accuse this man, because I have been abused by him both in my private life and my life as a subject of the state."

Lysias went on to explain the crimes Eratosthenes had committed as well as his role in the Thirty Tyrants' reign of terror. He touched on matters that were fresh in the memory of the public and the court. His testimony is characterized by an atmosphere of trust between orator and audience. Each knew what was at stake and realized the importance of making an extremely significant decision. Through Lycias's words, Athenian democracy itself recovered after

The so-called Venus of Arles, a Roman copy of a Greek statue of the goddess Aphrodite. The latter was influenced by the sculptor Praxiteles between 350 and 330 BC. Venus and Aphrodite are the same, the goddess of love.

Plato (429–347 BC) and Aristotle (384–322 BC)

Both Plato and Aristotle were opposed to the Sophists, itinerant teachers of philosophy, politics, and rhetoric. Noted for their skill in clever but fallacious argument, Sophists taught a persuasive rhetoric useful in public life, providing instruction for a fee. Plato and his disciple Aristotle considered them mercenary and objected to their view that truth and morality were matters of opinion. They countered the Sophists' relativism with an elaborate idealism.

They were equally opposed to the Cynics. Members of this school considered civilization and the external, material world contemptible, artificial, and unnatural. They advocated return to a simple, natural life, where happiness could be attained the only way possible, through self-sufficiency and independence. Plato countered their individualism with a new formula for an ideal society.

He considered only "the idea" as genuinely real, rejecting the view of empiricism, which contended that knowledge (including that based on scientific observation) is based on sense experience. Plato said the object of knowledge (the idea) had to be fixed, permanent, and unchangeable, based on reason, not sense perception. Reason results in certain intellectual insight, valid because its object is the eternal substance he called Form. Only it makes up the real world.

Once interested in a political career, Plato

what was termed the "white terror." Athens again was competent to judge, debate, and punish. Lysias concluded his testimony by alluding to the events of the revolution against the Thirty Tyrants: "You, judges, who have miraculously escaped death, tell me what would have come of you if democracy had not been restored! It takes more than one man to list everything the oligarchs have done to destroy the state. Witnesses to their actions are all around us: dismantled arsenals, wasted and desecrated temples,

grew disillusioned by the politics of Athens and turned to the philosophy of Socrates. He presented his own notions and interpretations of Socrates in the form of dialogues between the great philosopher and someone seeking truth through questions and answers. In 387 he founded the Academy in Athens, where Aristotle was his most important student. Applying his theory of knowledge to social philosophy, Plato wrote the *Republic* and the *Laws*. These described a *polis* (city) on earth resembling the ideal city-state, a blueprint for a state in which the philosophers-rulers exercise control over the two lower classes, peasant-artisans and soldiers. Because the leaders have true knowledge, there is no room for dissent. In 367 BC and 361 BC Plato tried unsuccessfully to interest the tyrant Dionysius II of Syracuse and his successor in putting his ideas into practice.

Although strongly influenced by Plato, Aristotle's philosophy developed in a different direction. Aristotle proposed an empirical, inductive approach rather than a deductive one, insisting that the senses and observation of visible reality were of great importance. He considered the role of the mind to be an important one. Aside from his strictly philosophical works on logic, ethics, and metaphysics, Aristotle left major scientific works on zoology, geography, ethnology, history, mathematics, and astronomy. Aristotle drew up an inventory of all existing political systems. His ideal polis combines the best elements of existing systems, ordered hierarchically by economic criteria and seniority, and run only by those with the means to permit free time for active participation in politics. Aristotle established his own school in Athens, the Lyceum. Although no direct political results can be demonstrated, his social philosophy may have influenced his student Alexander the Great.

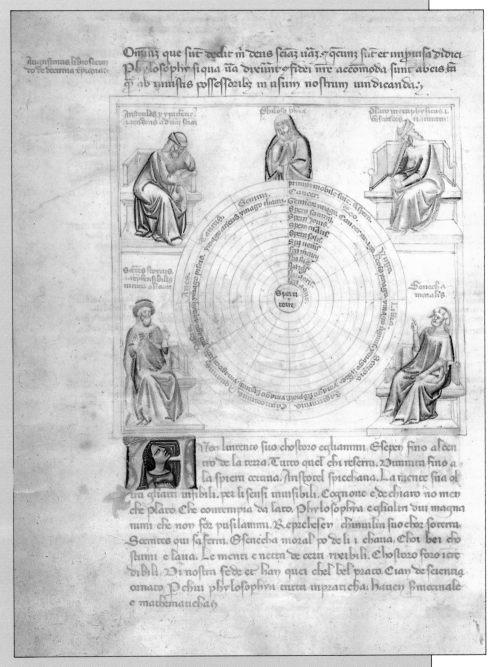

Italian manuscript from the fourteenth century showing the philosophers Socrates, Aristotle, Plato, and Seneca

exiled and murdered fellow citizens, corpses that never received a decent funeral. Yes, judges, these victims will rise up and ask you if you want to be an accessory to such horrors or if you will avenge such crimes! You have seen them, you have heard them; now, pronounce your verdict!"

Spartan Politics

The Lysias case illustrates the mood in Athens after the Peloponnesian War. It also throws light on Sparta's attitude after the final defeat of its perennial rival. Spartan dominance had catastrophic consequences in foreign relations. Sparta had gained its victory with the aid of the Persians. As a result, many Greek cities in Asia Minor had to cede their autonomy once again to Persia. The Persian War had been fought over this issue. Sparta forced a protectorate on other cities, making them pay considerable sums of money in tribute each year. In effect, Athenian imperialism (manifested in its domination of the Delian League and its own

Body armor, found in a Macedonian royal grave from the fourth century BC. It is made of iron and decorated with the royal emblems, a shining star and lion heads.

Greaves or shin protectors, found in a Macedonian royal grave. They are made of bronze, and are of unequal size telling us that one of the owner's legs was shorter than the other.

demands for annual tribute) had simply been replaced by Spartan imperialism.

The Spartans remained in rural Lacedaemon on the Peloponnese Peninsula, which was far too provincial for the role they had brought upon themselves. In that kingdom, society was divided into warriors and helots. Only the warriors were granted citizenship. There were originally two kings, both warriors.

Agesilaus II (c. 444–360 BC), King of Sparta (399–360 BC)

Sparta's most important leader during the first half of the fourth century BC was a man with a definite un-Spartan air: Agesilaus, who was chosen king in 399. Much is known about him from the writings of the historian Xenophon (431–355 BC), who was his friend and colleague. The king was small, frail, and had a slight limp. Such physical defects were close to insurmountable to a Spartan, whose country sent children born with any defects to the hills to die. Yet Agesilaus distinguished himself by his forthrightness and his piety and revealed himself as a major statesman and a general. After his coronation he opted for a similar course to the one Athens had followed earlier. He tried to free the Greek areas in Asia Minor from any dependence on Persia, emphasizing Greek superiority in all physical and spiritual aspects to foster a sense of cultural identity. Whoever appealed to Sparta for protection, he said, could always count on the full commitment of all Spartans. In 399 BC, he sent an army to the coast of Asia Minor in an effort to halt Persian raids. His campaigns around the Bosporus and the Meander River valley between 396 and 394 BC were, to some degree, a foretaste of Alexander the Great's battles against Persia. Although he could never have hoped for complete victory, his successes there revealed the advanced state of decline of the Persian Empire. In the fourth century, it no longer presented a threat to Greece. Persia's only remaining influence was financial. It used its wealth to stoke internal fights and quarrels among the Greek city-states. When Agesilaus turned Sparta against Persia, it tried to pit other states against Spartan rule. Some of these sought assistance from Persia.

The Corinthian War: 395–387 BC

In 395 BC, Athens, Argos, Corinth, and Thebes allied against Sparta. The Spartan army was forced to give up its campaign against Persia to deal with this threat. Sparta, to counter the coalition, allied with Persia. The eight-year conflict, called the Corinthian War, ended in 387 BC. The Persians' divide-and-conquer politics were so successful that the Persian king, Artaxerxes II (404–359 BC), was able to dictate the peace terms of the Peace of Antalcidas, called the King's Peace, on its unwilling subject states. By the terms of this Persian-Spartan settlement, the entire west coast of Asia Minor was ceded to Persia and the city-states of Greece were made autonomous. Persia benefited most from this because it finally brought the Ionian cities under Persian sovereignty. Peace actually meant defeat to all Spartan ambitions and the end of Spartan dominance. This left Athens free to develop its position as a wealthy trading town, maintaining its status as the foremost cultural center in the Greek world. Although it would never again play a major role in Greek politics, there was a definite Athenian renaissance.

The Ascendancy of Thebes: 382–362 BC

Almost a hundred years earlier, the Athenian orator Isocrates (436-338 BC) had hoped to unite all Greeks in one nation because of their shared repugnance for Persia. Panhellenism had been a favorite topic of discussion. The drive toward Greek unity under Athens had gained momentum. In the meantime, others began to wonder about domination by a state rising rapidly under a capable leader named Epaminondas. The city was Thebes, centrally located in Greece and allied with Athens for some time.

In 382 BC, in spite of the King's Peace, Sparta invaded Thebes, evidently taking the initiative before that city-state gained further power. Thebes sought and got the support of Athens. In 379 BC the Thebian general Pelopidas led a rebellion that managed to drive out the Spartans. Full-scale war resumed. Epaminondas introduced new bat-

One of the successful strategies of the army of King Philip of Macedonia was attacking the enemy with *phalanxes* (heavily armed infantry in close ranks). Each warrior in such phalanx was armed with a lance and a short sword, and wore a helmet, a round shield, and shin protectors. This reconstruction shows a phalanx charging against the enemy in closed formation.

Bust of Isocrates, a Roman copy from a Greek original that dates from the fourth century BC

The Philippeion in
Olympia, a round monument
that was started during the
reign of Philip II of
Macedonia after the battle of
Chaeronea (338 BC).
Presumably, it was finished
in Alexander the Great's
time. In the Philippeion were
statues of Philip, his wife
Olympias, his parents, and his
son Alexander.

Bust that is probably
a portrait of Philip II of
Macedonia.
It was made between
350 and 325 BC.

610

tle tactics for the traditional phalanx formation. They brought spectacular results at the
battle of Leuctra in 371 BC. Thebes resound-
ingly defeated Sparta, finally ending its pre-
eminence in Greece. Thebes moved to first
place among the Greek city-states. Its dominance was widely resented and short-lived,
however. Athens and Sparta joined forces
against the common enemy in 369 BC, ultimately defeating the Theban army in the
Battle of Mantinea in 362 BC. Many had
hoped that Epaminondas would unite Greece
and forge it into a close-knit nation, but he
was among those who died in the battle.

The Rise of Macedonia

In a speech delivered in 380 BC, the orator
Isocrates put into words the sentiments of the
inhabitants of Athens at the time. He noted
that Athens was the favorite city of the gods,
that the gods had granted it victory in its
fight against the Persians, and that Athens
was tutor to the rest of Greece. Only this city
produced and nurtured democracy, and

ended the era of lawlessness and tyranny. Only here were the fine arts perfected and passed down to succeeding generations. Athenian tolerance and love of freedom were so great that all strangers were admitted to the city and allowed to make their fortunes. Exiles and the persecuted were taken in with hospitality. Only at the end of his oratory does Isocrates tell his audience why he speaks of Athens with such praise. Precisely because Athens is Greece's most fortunate city, it must see to it that the Greeks unite under Athenian leadership. This plan would be realized, but in modified form, by Alexander the Great fifty years later.

During the decade of Theban dominance (371–362 BC), two Macedonian princes were held as hostages in Thebes. One of them was to become Philip II, king of Macedonia and father of Alexander the Great. Philip was born in 382 BC, became king in 359 BC, and was murdered in 336 BC.

"Such a man!" the Greek orator Demosthenes said after Philip's death. "Such an enemy we had to fight in the person of this Philip. He gave up everything just to get power; even his arms and legs and his health. He was willing to sacrifice everything to gain fame and glory." Demosthenes understood there was a great danger lurking in the primitive, rough region of Macedonia that produced men such as Philip. Unlike

Gold coin from
Tarsus, most likely a portrait
of Philip II of Macedonia   611

Isocrates, he rejected a strong monarchy as a solution to Greek unity. He incessantly warned the Athenian people of the menacing presence of Macedonia. If they were not watchful, it would crush them, if not immediately, then ten or fifteen years hence.

When the rumor spread in Athens that Philip was seriously ill, Demosthenes called out to his fellow citizens: "Did Philip die? No, he is merely ill. And his illness is insignificant, because even if Philip dies, your sluggishness would cause another Philip to rise up." Demosthenes's rage was inspired not only by the continuously advancing Macedonian armies that were uncomfortably close to Attica; he also viewed the loss of the colonies along the Black Sea as a stain on Athens's reputation. This had been Philip's doing when he cleaned up the last remnants of the once-proud empire. In his now-famous oratories against Philip of Macedonia (called the *Philippics*), Demosthenes becomes increasingly vehement against the military usurper from the north.

Demosthenes's opponent was a colleague and orator by the name of Aeschines, who acted as the spokesman for the pro-Macedonian party. In the end, Demosthenes succeeded in marginalizing Aeschines and his pro-Macedonian movement and pushed for an alliance with Thebes. But the alliance came too late and was not strong enough to stop the Macedonians. On August 7, 338 BC, Philip of Macedonia, with his army of 30,000 foot soldiers and 2,000 horsemen, defeated the somewhat smaller army of the Greek allies near Chaeronea on the Boeotian Plain. The classical age of Greece had come to an end. Within a few years, Greece and the world would have changed unrecognizably as the result of the lightning strikes of another Macedonian, Alexander the Great. In the meantime (340 BC), in southern Italy, an insignificant peasant village called Rome was steadily and doggedly expanding its influence.

The Lion of Chaeronea,
a statue on the mass grave for
the Thebans who died
during the battle of Chaeronea
(338 BC)

Portrait of Alexander the Great (probably a Roman copy), a man who became a veritable living legend. His father was King Philip of Macedonia, who arranged for Aristotle himself to become his son's teacher. When Alexander was twenty-two years old, he inherited a realm of modest size, but after some successful campaigns, he ruled an enormous empire.

Alexander the Great

Conqueror of the Ancient World

The Macedonian prince Alexander crossed the Hellespont (called the Dardanelles today) when he was scarcely twenty-two years old. By the time he succumbed to fever at the age of thirty-three, he had managed to move the eastern frontier of his empire all the way to India, conquering tens of millions of people. His own personality turned out to be the only binding force in his short-lived empire.

Within a few years of his death, his generals divided the vast territory among themselves. Alexander had come on like a whirlwind and passed as quickly. After his swift campaigns, nothing would be the same. He had expanded the Greek world far beyond the Mediterranean, yet details of his life are shrouded in legend. The chronicling of history at that time was often primarily a literary genre; ac-

Terra-cotta statuette of
two chatting ladies, that was
a grave gift from the
third century BC. It was found
in Myrina, Asia Minor
(present-day Turkey).

Cameo (portrait cut
out of a gemstone) that
probably depicts Alexander
the Great and his mother
Olympias

tual fact took second place. Many historians
did not bother to investigate the legends they
heard or read, but simply copied them, pre-
senting them as genuine. Furthermore, they
frequently defended the viewpoint of one of
Alexander's successors. The result is that
almost nothing has come down firsthand.
Most sources on Alexander actually date
only to Roman times. Arrian (second century AD), his most reliable biographer, lived
more than four hundred years after him, at
the time of the Roman emperor Hadrian.

Alexander's Childhood

Alexander was born in Pella, capital of
Macedonia, the son of its king Philip II and
Olympias, princess of Epirus. Philip had met
her when he was initiated into the local reli-
gious mysteries of the island of Samothrace.
Philip sent for the Athenian philosopher
Aristotle to complete his son's education in

rhetoric, philosophy, literature, and science. Apparently, they were inspiring master and apt student.

The Greek biographer Plutarch writes: "It is clear that Alexander inherited from Aristotle his love of medicine. When his friends were ill, he would prescribe treatments and medication, as shown in his letters. Alexander was an avid reader and Onesicritus relates that Alexander would go to bed with a copy of the *Iliad* that had been corrected by Aristotle. He would place it under his headrest next to his dagger. Later, when he visited the Asian interior, he ordered his treasurer Harpalus to send books from the west. Harpalus sent Philistus's history of Sicily, the plays of Euripides, Sophocles, and Aeschylus, and dithyrambs by Telestes and Philoxenus."

Domestic Battles

Philip II was assassinated in the summer of 336 BC. Alexander ascended the throne and, with the aid of his mother Olympias (who had a long and bloody career in Macedonian politics in her own right), he had the conspirators summarily executed. He was beset by rivals at home and rebels abroad, but the old general Antipater swayed the army on Alexander's behalf. This enabled him to take command. In Thessaly, leaders of an independence movement had taken over the government. Alexander threw them out and reasserted Macedonian rule. Epirus was already tied to Macedonia through dynastic ties. By the end of the summer, Alexander was elected king by a Panhellenic conference at Corinth, although he could not count on the support of the Greek city-states south of Thermopylae. They had been forced to recognize him after a battle at Chaeronea, but it was clear they would not pass up an opportunity to oust a king they considered a barbarian.

Alexander crossed the northern border the next year, in command of Greek forces against the Persians, carrying out a plan against rebellious Thracians originally outlined by his father. The successful campaign took five months overall, extending to the Danube River. Once returned, he took only a week to subdue rebelling Illyrians. There was rebellion, as well, in Thebes, incited by the orator Demosthenes and funded by Persian gold. The rebels spread the rumor that the Macedonian king had died and then they attacked the Macedonian garrison that occupied their citadel. Alexander learned of their actions, and having reached an agreement with his adversaries in the north, moved his army rapidly southward, in forced marches. The king, presumed dead, sudden-

ly appeared before the walls of Thebes and took the city by storm. He razed it, sparing only the temples and the house of the famous Greek poet Pindar. He sold the surviving inhabitants, some 8,000 of them, into slavery. The speed and harshness of this retaliation so impressed the other Greeks

that they surrendered almost immediately. Alexander treated the other rebellious cities with greater leniency, demanding only the extradition of ten rebel leaders, including Demosthenes, from the city of Athens. Demosthenes then said that his extradition would be as unwise as the decision by a herd of sheep to buy off the wolf by offering him the shepherd dog. The popular assembly sent negotiators to Alexander, who managed to talk him out of the extradition. The ten leaders of the rebellion remained in Athens and persisted in their opposition, albeit less overtly.

Bust of Aristotle, Alexander's teacher. The statue is a Roman copy of a Greek original that dates from c. 330 BC.

615

The King and His Army

Alexander stood on the shores of the Hellespont with an army comprising 30,000 foot soldiers and some 5,000 horsemen. These formed the core units of the army and were composed primarily of Macedonians and Thessalians. There were also a great number of Macedonians among the infantry. However, at least half of it consisted of mercenaries drawn from the rest of the Greek world, from Thrace, and from regions farther north. These entered the service of the party, offering them the greatest reward. Military service provided pay and a share in the booty, although the soldier had to bring his own equipment. Alexander was also surrounded by his personal retinue, called *hetairoi*, or comrades-in-arms. This hetairoi squadron of 1,500 consisted mainly of Macedonian men from the higher classes. Alexander was their direct boss and wherever he appeared and whatever he did, his hetairoi were always near. This retinue was customary in Macedonian society. The king

Bronze statue of Alexander the Great on horseback during the battle of Granicus, that was found in Herculaneum. It is a Roman copy made in the first century BC, after a Greek original by Lysippus, the Macedonian court sculptor, from c. 330 BC.

regarded its members as on equal footing with him, treating them as friends and allowing them liberties not granted others.

Alexander did not encounter much difficulty in assembling his army. The peace forged by him and his father in Greece had caused a slump in the mercenary business. Looking for their fortunes elsewhere, numerous soldiers had already crossed the Aegean Sea to join some Persian troop contingents. In every one of his battles against the Persians, Alexander would face opposing Greek mercenaries. Many of them defected to his army, not from patriotism but because they expected higher earnings. Alexander frequently lambasted the Greeks fighting on the Persian side as traitors of the Greek cause, a Panhellenic concept certainly not shared by the mercenaries involved.

Alexander's foot soldiers advanced in *phalanx* formation, that is, a battle line of heavily armed soldiers, a formation that had been in use long before Philip and Alexander. The Macedonians adapted it by extending the wings of the rear lines some fifteen feet (4.6 meters), thus causing the wings of the first five rows to form a closed front. The phalanx now advanced like a gigantic slow-moving porcupine across the battlefield, or stood still in an even tighter defensive position. If the formation became confused, all was lost: it was impossible to restore the battle array in the heat of battle. Generally, the phalanx was able to resist an attack by the cavalry. For that reason, it was always placed at the center of the battle array, with the more mobile, lightly armed infantry and the cavalry at the sides. Alexander exploited the flexibility of this army to great advantage. It brought him victory after victory.

The Battle of Granicus River

Alexander took two years to consolidate the position he had inherited. In the spring of 334 BC, matters at home were sufficiently secure for him to attempt crossing into Asia Minor. He led his army of 35,000 Macedonians and Greeks across the Hellespont, leaving Antipater behind as regent in Pella. Near Troy at the Granicus River in northwestern Asia Minor, he attacked an army of Persians and Greeks, 40,000 strong, winning the battle and reputedly losing only 110 soldiers of his own. The road to Asia Minor lay open and Alexander had little resistance to fear.

After Xerxes's death in 424, the kingdom of Persia had declined rapidly. Under ineffective kings, the *satraps* (provincial gover-

The remains of late fourth-century houses in Pella, Macedonia, the place where Alexander the Great was born in 356 BC

617

ΔΑΡΕΙΟΣ

ΠΕΡΣΑΙ

Darius I, king of Persia,
is sitting in the midst of a multitude
of Persians and all kinds of animals.
This picture is painted on a huge terra-cotta
krater (vessel in which water and wine were mixed),
and was made by the so-called Darius-painter in
the third quarter of the fourth century BC.

nors) had actually divided Persia into a series
of semiindependent principalities. Artaxerxes (reigned 358–338 BC), the predeces-
sor of the reigning king, Darius III (reigned
335–330 BC), had restored Persian hegemony in the cities of Susa and Persepolis with
brute force. Many Persians might have considered Alexander's arrival a liberation.

Greek mercenaries, he moved the battle to Greek territory. If he had not died of illness in 333 BC, Alexander's story might have been very different.

The victory at the Granicus had a lasting effect. When Alexander's army approached the Persian government center of Sardis, long able to withstand other attacks, the satrap walked through the gate to surrender. One by one, all Greek colonies but Memnon's fell to Macedonian hands. It took Alexander barely a year to establish hegemony in Asia Minor.

The Gordian Knot

Alexander passed through the holy Phrygian capital Gordion on his route of conquest. According to Greek mythology, Gordius, the king of Phrygia and the father of the Phrygian national hero Minos, had tied the pole of his wagon to its yoke with a rope of bark. Gordius, a Phrygian peasant, had been made king because he fulfilled an oracle that said the first person to enter town driving a wagon must be made ruler. The grateful king dedicated his wagon to Zeus, tying it in a grove in the god's temple with a complex knot. The knot was so difficult no one could undo it. It was said that anyone who could untie it would rule all of Asia. Alexander unsheathed his sword and cut the knot in half. He was rewarded with booty sufficient to cover his campaign expenses. (The act has given rise to the expressions *a Gordian knot*, referring to a complex problem, and *to cut the Gordian knot*, meaning to achieve a swift solution.)

The Battle of Issus

Moving on south in 333, Alexander initially passed by and then turned around to fight the huge Persian army at the Battle of Issus in Syria, close to the Mediterranean. It was catastrophic for the Persians, while the Macedonians suffered relatively minor losses. The weakling Persian king, Darius III, fled, leaving his mother, wife, and children behind. Alexander ordered them all treated with the respect normally accorded royalty. He was already beginning his efforts to placate conquered peoples in order to build a socially integrated empire.

The Conquest of Tyre

After Issus, Syria offered no resistance. Only the well-fortified Phoenician seaport of Tyre put up a fight. Although willing to acknowledge Alexander as king, it was not prepared to let him enter the island on which it lay. Alexander besieged it for seven months in 332, finally seizing and razing it in a bloodbath. He had the women and children sold as

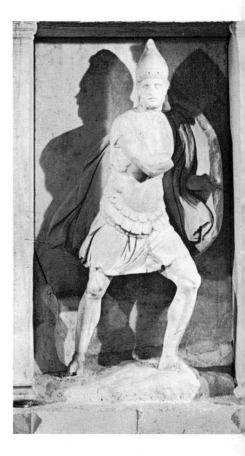

Stone grave monument of Aristonautes, here depicted in the armor of a Greek soldier. It was found in the Kerameikos cemetery near Athens, and dates from c. 320 BC.

Persian defense lines depended on a few powerful soldiers. One of them was the Greek mercenary Memnon. He had advised his superiors to let Alexander go bankrupt and to apply scorched-earth tactics in Asia Minor (burning the land as they retreated). Memnon was a formidable opponent. Aided by Persian money, Phoenician ships, and

slaves. Darius, already deeply affected by the Persian defeat at Issus, offered Alexander his lands up to the Euphrates River, his daughter in marriage, and a large dowry in exchange for friendship and peace after the fall of Tyre. As guarantee of his good intentions, he offered to send his son as a hostage. Alexander responded that he already had whatever Darius could offer and that he would marry the daughter regardless of her father's permission. He announced that he would come to take what he considered his, but not immediately.

Farther down the coast, the fortress at Gaza offered resistance. It took a long siege to break the city. Because Alexander was injured during it, he exacted terrible revenge. Jerusalem, however, surrendered without a single blow exchanged. The high priest in full regalia came to welcome the conqueror and his army.

The Conquest of Egypt

Later the same year, Alexander led his army down the eastern Mediterranean shore and across the Sinai Peninsula into Egypt. He was welcomed everywhere as a liberator. Fighting was hardly necessary. He founded the city of Alexandria (named for him) on the Mediterranean at the mouth of the Nile. It would become the commercial and cultural center of the Greek world. He would later found scores of other Alexandrias to accommodate his veteran soldiers. He continued west along the North African coast, subjugating Cyrene, capital of the kingdom of Cyrenaica, with little resistance.

Pilgrimage to the Oracle of Amon-Re

In 331 BC, Alexander traveled to the oracle of Amon-Re, Egyptian god of the sun, at Siwa oasis in the Libyan desert. At about this time, he had begun to stress the notion that he was descended from the gods. The Egyptians, who looked upon Alexander as their pharaoh, did not attempt to dissuade him from the idea. Egyptian pharaohs were traditionally considered sons of Amon-Re. The Greeks identified Amon-Re with Zeus and held the oracle in great renown. Alexander sought the same linkage. After the pilgrimage, Alexander called himself a son of Zeus. The Greeks had no difficulty

Two griffins guarding the entrance gate to the palace of Persepolis, the residence of King Darius III. Alexander conquered Persepolis in 324 BC.

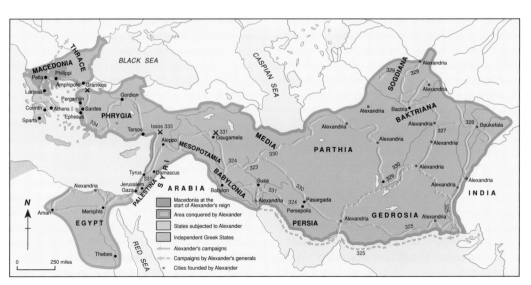

The realm of Alexander the Great

620

with this concept, especially not where it involved a young man with military achievements so extraordinary as to appear superhuman. Whatever else, he was surely a remarkable man and most Greeks and Egyptians were willing to treat him as a god.

Battle of Gaugamela

Once he had secured the Mediterranean coast, Alexander turned his attention north and east. In 331 BC he retraced his steps across the Sinai Peninsula and up through Palestine to Babylon, with an army of 40,000 infantry and 7,000 cavalry. They crossed first the Euphrates and then the Tigris Rivers. East of the Tigris, Darius waited for him with an army of a million, according to legend. Its contingents came from all over the Persian Empire and included Indians with elephants. Alexander routed it near the town of Gaugamela in northern Mesopotamia on

October 1, 331 BC. Babylon surrendered. Darius and his troops fled before the Macedonian as Alexander conquered the city of Susa, which held the treasury of the Persian Empire, then Persepolis, a Persian capital, and, finally, the city of Pasargadae. Legend says that Alexander burned Persepolis in a fit of drunkenness. The conquest of Mesopotamia had become reality.

The "Usurper" Bessus

Darius had essentially already forfeited the throne. He was murdered in 330 BC by a conspiracy of satraps in the northwest. One of them, Bessus, proclaimed himself king. Alexander viewed himself as successor and branded the satraps as regicides and usurpers. Whether this is a justified claim is uncertain. The Persian Empire was fighting a life-and-death struggle against a foreign invader. The king had not offered proper

The dangerous Hindu Kush pass in eastern Afghanistan, one of the passes over which Alexander started his conquest of the Indus Valley. He crossed this harsh region with his army as many as three times.

621

The famous Alexander mosaic (second century BC), found in the House of the Faun in Pompeii. The picture shows the confrontation between Alexander the Great *(left)* and Darius *(in his cart on the right)* during the battle of Gaugamela in which they fought each other. It copies a famous fourth-century BC painting.

The so-called *Mars Ludovisii*, a Roman copy of a statue of the god Ares. It was probably made by Lysippus, the court sculptor of Alexander the Great, in the late fourth century BC.

leadership. The Persian Empire had collapsed over a short period of time. Bessus and a few other prominent Persians had mounted a final effort to save their country, even killing their "divine" king when he became an obstacle to that objective. To them, his murder was no doubt viewed as a necessity. Bessus unleashed a popular war, forcing Alexander to battle ferociously the Persians. They preferred burning their land to surrendering it to the invader. Bessus was betrayed, taken by Alexander, and executed as a traitor and usurper. The huge complex of Persepolis was burned to the ground, a symbol of the decline of Persian power.

The Central Asian Campaign

Alexander set out on a new campaign in 329 BC to complete his conquest over the full range of the former Persian Empire, including the provinces of western India. Between 329 and 327 BC, he broke the last traces of resistance in Central Asia. His realm now ranged from Media and Parthia near the southern shores of the Caspian Sea (today's Iran, Afghanistan, and Baluchistan) and the northern regions of Bactria and Sogdiana (modern Turkmenistan).

India, the Final Campaign

In the fall of 327 BC, Alexander reached the Indus Valley by way of the Hindu Kush and the Valley of Kabul. This was a new world. Although the campaign went smoothly, the troops began to grumble. Rumors circulated that they still had far to go until they conquered the world, which was their general's stated goal. The Indian expedition demonstrated to all that Alexander wanted more than just to conquer the Persian Empire. He wanted to unite under his rule the entire inhabited world as it was then known to the Greeks. The army crossed the Indus River in 326 BC, penetrating the Punjab as far as the Hyphasis River. Here the troops mutinied, refusing to proceed. They wanted to go home. Alexander gave up the effort to conquer the rest of India and farther east. Like the nomads of Central Asia, the peoples to the east would not be included in his empire. Their absence from the tapestry of a realm that encompassed nearly the entire known world would not be widely noticed. Alexander was forced to compromise; he could not continue without any army. He had a fleet built and sailed down the Indus River, reaching its mouth in 325 BC. The fleet

The River Indus, that formed the eastern border of the realm that Alexander conquered

Part of the decorations of the facade of the Persian royal palace in Susa, also conquered by Alexander. It is made of glazed tiles and dates from the fifth century BC.

623

sailed on to the Persian Gulf. Alexander and the army went west by land along the arid coastline to Media. The fleet was expected to sail along parallel to their line of travel, supplying the army with food and water. Because the ships were unable to sail against the prevailing winds, the army was forced to forage for itself in the desert. Here, Alexander lost more men than in all his battles combined.

Alexander's Imperial Integration

All along his line of conquest, Alexander

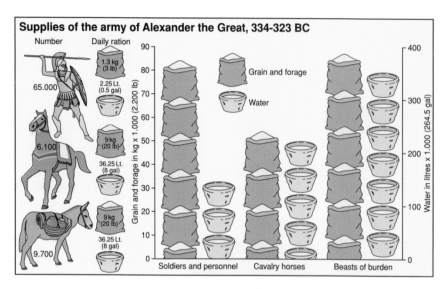

Supplies of the army of Alexander the Great, 334–323 BC

Number — Daily ration

65.000 — 1.3 kg (3 lb); 2.25 Lt. (0.5 gal)

6.100 — 9 kg (20 lb); 36.25 Lt. (8 gal)

9.700 — 9 kg (20 lb); 36.25 Lt. (8 gal)

Grain and forage in kg × 1.000 (2.200 lb)

Grain and forage

Water

Water in litres × 1.000 (264.5 gal)

Soldiers and personnel — Cavalry horses — Beasts of burden

Supplies of the army of Alexander the Great. In order to keep an army this size in proper condition, good organization was needed, if only to get enough food. Every day the army needed 250 tons (225,000 kilograms) of cereals and 190,000 gallons (720,000 liters) of water.

The marble Alexander *sarcophagus* (a stone coffin) from Sidon. This grave monument was probably made for Abdalonymus, the king of Sidon, who was placed on his throne by Alexander (333–332 BC). The coffin is decorated with scenes from Alexander's life.

founded cities, most of which he named Alexandria. He had them well constructed, paved, supplied with water, and settled with Greek veterans. The cities served as magnets to merchants and scholars alike, attracting the creators of a new economy and a new Hellenistic intelligentsia. They established and extended Greek culture and language.

In 324 BC, when Alexander returned to Susa to attend to the affairs of state, it was evident that he intended to create a mixed Macedonian-Persian elite that would hold his empire together. In an effort to reconcile the conquerors and the conquered, he had Darius, last of the Achaemenids, buried with his forefathers in a respectful ceremony. As his successor on the Persian throne, Alexander wore the vestments and insignia of the king of kings. He ruled from the residences of Susa and Pasargadae, which had been spared in the war. He adopted Persian customs and took Persian wives, organizing a mass marriage ceremony of Macedonian men with Persian women in Susa. He himself married the oldest daughter of Darius, Barsine (also called Stateira; she died about 323 BC), and another Persian woman, Roxana, the daughter of Oxyartes of Sogdiana (she died about 311 BC). He appointed Persians to important offices and drafted thousands of young Persians into his army, forming new regiments of infantry.

These actions, as well as his showing himself off as the Persian king, caused great tension between Alexander and his entourage and the Macedonians, in particular his hetairoi. When the new Iranian troops were called up at the same time that Macedonian veterans were dismissed, the veterans mutinied. Alexander still had sufficient leverage to realize a dramatic reconciliation with the rebels, celebrated with a banquet for the entire army. Here he openly prayed to the gods for "unity and equally shared rule" between Macedonians and Persians.

Alexander's mortality became apparent soon after his command that he be worshiped. In the spring of 323 BC, he went to Babylon. In June, he came down with a fever and died two weeks later at the age of thirty-three. He had bequeathed his empire "to the strongest," setting off a struggle that would last fifty years. His sense of his own divinity was no doubt fostered, as well, by his extraordinary military success. One of the greatest commanders and strategists in history, he had, indeed, conquered a vast part of the world in an incredibly short period of time. His efforts to spread the civilization of Greece and to combine the heritage of Persia and Macedonia at least set the stage for the Hellenistic kingdoms that followed.

Bronze statue of Tyche of Antioch. The Greeks saw the goddess Tyche as the personification of Fortune or Fate. Many Greek cities had their own Tyche (in this case the city of Antioch). By worshiping her they hoped to influence the future of the city.

Hellenism

The Battle of the Diadochs

When Alexander died in 323 BC, at the age of thirty-three, he left behind a power vacuum. Roxana, one of his two Persian wives, did not give birth to his son Alexander until four weeks after the king's death. The infant's half-brother, Aridaeus, was rumored to be mentally deficient and physically unwell. Both the newborn Alexander and Aridaeus were invested with imperial titles, Alexander IV and Philip III. Since neither was in a position to exercise power, it fell into the hands of the imperial regent Perdiccas, who divided it among the commanders of Alexander's army. They are known to history as the *diadochoi* (Greek for successors) or diadochs. At first the empire preserved a precarious unity, while each diadoch attempted to secure for himself as

Bronze statue
of Silenos,
the companion of
the Greek god
Dionysus

much of its wealth as possible, but eventually they fell into open conflict. Years of war ensued, each marked by the formation of fresh coalitions. Some time later, in 317 and 310 BC respectively, Aridaeus and Alexander IV were both murdered, and there was no longer any lawful successor to stand in the way of the diadochs' ambitions.

Ptolemy I, called Ptolemy Soter (The Preserver) (c. 367–283 BC)

Ptolemy was a talented captain in Alexander's army who proved to be a skilled politician. Appointed diadoch in charge of the *satrapies* (provinces) of Egypt and Libya in 323 BC, he used the position as a power base. For almost twenty years he battled the other diadochs, consolidating and expanding his realm. He successfully fended off invasions of Egypt and the Mediterranean island of Rhodes but was unable to take over Cyprus and some of Greece. Ptolemy I expanded Alexandria, making it the largest Greek settlement in the known world. He founded the great Alexandrian library.

Ptolemy had Alexander's body diverted to Egypt, though the king was known to have preferred the oasis of Siwa as his final rest-

The altar of Zeus of Pergamon, dating from the first half of the second century BC. The altar is now in the Pergamon Museum in Berlin, Germany.

ing place. Ptolemy had the body, which was given divine honors, brought first to Memphis and then to Alexandria, where he placed it in a golden coffin. In 305 BC Ptolemy proclaimed himself king of Egypt. Before he abdicated in favor of one of his younger sons in 285 BC, he had expanded the kingdom to include Palestine and Cyrenaica. The dynasty he established, the Ptolemies, would rule Egypt until the arrival of the Romans in 31 BC.

The Antigonids

Other notable figures among the many diadochs include the old Antigonus Monophthalmus (One-Eye) and his son Demetrius Poliorcetes (Taker of Cities), so-called for his skill in laying sieges. Antigonus was already an old man when Alexander crossed the Hellespont. He was left behind as governor of the recently conquered Asia Minor when the king went on to other conquests. He immediately seized the opportunity offered by Alexander's death, sharing power with his son. Advocating the preservation of the unity of the empire, Antigonus and Demetrius found themselves in permanent conflict with the other dia-

dochs. They were very successful in warfare and, in 306 BC they became the first diadochs to call themselves kings.

Five years later Antigonus was killed in a battle against a coalition of the other

Portrait of Mithridates VI, dating from the first quarter of the first century BC. The style of the portrait is influenced by the portraits of Alexander the Great.

627

diadochs. Demetrius withdrew to Greece, where he held out for a considerable time as king of Macedonia and Thessaly. However, in 286 BC he was captured and imprisoned by the diadoch Seleucus. He died in prison in 283 BC. Demetrius's son, Antigonus Gonatas, eventually managed to regain possession of the Macedonian throne and to extend his authority over Greece. His descendants, the Antigonids, remained in power until the Romans put an end to their kingdom.

The Seleucids

Seleucus, the founder of the Seleucid dynasty, had his original power base in Mesopotamia and the countries farther east. He gradually expanded his influence to the west, establishing as his capital a new city he had built in Syria. He named it Antioch, after his father Antiochus. It grew to become the most important metropolis in Asia, though never as great as Alexandria of the Ptolemies in the realm of culture. His territory comprised all that had been conquered by Alexander, except the possessions of the Ptolemies, the old Macedonia, Greece, and the parts of India lost to the Indian prince

Alexandria

Alexandria stood out as more than a *polis*, a *megalopolis* (a thickly populated region centering on a metropolis) as well as a royal residence. It was the most important city in the eastern Mediterranean, founded by the sea, in 331 BC by Alexander the Great, on the west side of the Nile Delta. The city was probably conceived as a military support point, but it very rapidly also became the trading and administrative center of Egypt under the Greeks. Alexandria was the first polis to take its name from a historical founder. Alexander may have founded the city in a very concrete sense, for it was he who is said to have laid out the grid system of the city plan. It is characteristic of the imperial character of the time—a city founded by a ruler who gave it his name and determined its shape. Even if he did not design the city himself, he is one of a long line of kings and popes who determined, through their ideas and patronage of architects and engineers, the urban fabrics of cities and centers throughout Europe, North Africa, and the East.

Alexandria had a great number of important public buildings, including the royal palace of the Ptolemies and, connected to it, the famous *Mouseion* and its library. The Mouseion was simultaneously a temple of the Muses and a research institute where scholars and artists could devote themselves to learning and art at the ruler's expense, advancing science, engineering, music, and the visual arts. A vital part of the city was its great harbor. There, in the third century BC,

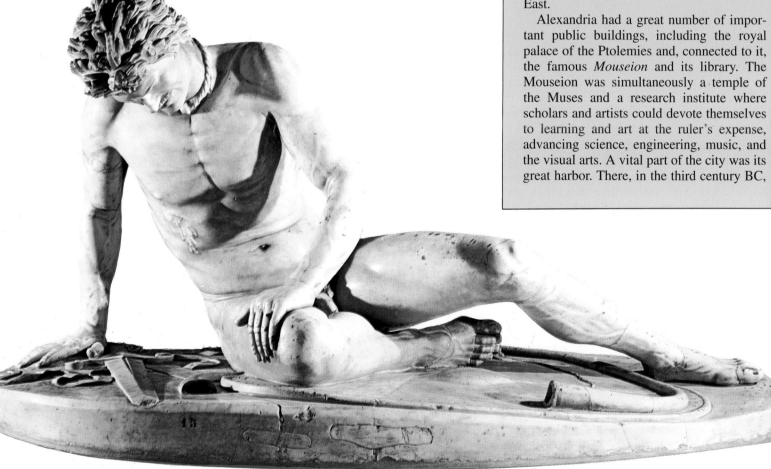

A Gaul is mortally wounded in a battle with diadochs. This Roman marble copy of a Greek bronze statue dating from 230–220 BC is in the Capitoline Museum in Rome.

the *pharos*, or lighthouse, became one of the wonders of the ancient world. Alexandria exported various products manufactured by Alexandrian craftspeople, including linen, papyrus, and precious metalwork. However, it was also important as a transit port for Egyptian grain and wares from India, Arabia, and even more distant countries, which arrived in Egypt by way of the Red Sea and the caravan routes.

Life in Alexandria was exciting. The Greek poet Theocritus gives us two women, Praxinoë and Gorgon, on their way to a procession:

Gorgon: I was a fool to come and fetch you! I was almost crushed by the crowd and the horses. Why in God's name did you choose to live so far away?

Praxinoë: That crazy husband of mine made me come here. It's more suitable here for chicken coops than for houses. And it's simply to prevent the two of us from being neighbors. The bastard is always jealous.

Gorgon: Don't talk so loud when the child's right here. Don't you see how he's looking at you? Now, listen, darling, we don't have anything against your daddy.

They go out. Theocritus describes the pushing, shouting, and swearing of the crowd as it presses forward so as not to miss anything.

Praxinoë: Oh, heavens! What a lot of people! It's worse than an anthill! Look, there's the king's horse! Don't knock me flat, sir. What a gorgeous animal! Hey, don't do that, I say!

As the center of the empire of the Ptolemies, Alexandria participated in the decline of that empire after the end of the third century. Sharper social contrasts, dwindling prosperity, political unrest and friction among the various ethnic groups did not spare Alexandria. But even under Roman rule, Alexandria continued to be the undisputed capitol of Egypt, a trade center of the first rank and, when the time came, one of the most important focal points of Christianity.

Cameo, probably depicting Ptolemy II and his wife and sister Arsinoé II. The Egyptian tradition of kings marrying their sisters was accepted by the Greeks.

Chandragupta. In effect, Seleucus ruled from Sardis to Kabul. In 305 or 304 BC, he, too, proclaimed himself a king.

In the huge territory of the Seleucids many nations spoke many languages and adhered to many ways of life. The empire, unable to achieve sustainable integration, gradually crumbled under Seleucus's successors. Rebels within and enemies without eroded its imperial power. In the east, Bactria made itself virtually independent under its own Greek rulers. In northern Persia, the warlike Parthians roamed at will, ultimately conquering many of the eastern provinces. Seleucid rule was shaky. Clever usurpers set up their own kingdoms in imperial territory. One such state was Pergamon, on the Aegean Sea, run from the city of the same name. The Jewish guerilla fighter Judas Maccabaeus is perhaps the most famous opponent of the Seleucids.

Judas Maccabaeus (died 161 BC)

Although he was one of the Jewish family named Hasmonaean, the Latin surname of Judas Maccabaeus probably derived from Aramaic *maqqabâ* (the Hammerer). It gave rise to the English *Maccabee*, applied to his relatives. Palestine had been seized from the Ptolemies by Antioch. In 168 BC, the Seleucid king Antiochus IV Epiphanes outlawed Judaism and ordered the worship of Greek gods, persecuting anyone who remained true to Jewish religion and culture.

Mattathias, patriarch of the Hasmonaeans, not only objected, he killed a government official and a Jew who had complied with the order. In 167 BC, he fled to the mountains with his five sons and a loyal band of Jews, initiating a lengthy revolt against the Seleucids. After he died in 161 BC his son Judas took command of the rebellion, defeating much larger Syrian armies between 166 and 165 BC. His restoration of Jewish rites to the Temple of Jerusalem (December 165 BC) is commemorated by the Jewish festival Hanukkah.

The temple of Apollo in Didyma (building was started in c. 300 BC), seen from the inside. Normally the ceremonial stairs would be used as an entrance, but in this case visitors had to enter through two tunnels on the left and right of the stair. This unusual way of entering a temple must undoubtedly have put any seeking Apollo, the god of oracles, in the right mood.

Antipater (c. 398–319 BC)

As soon as news of Alexander's death reached Greece in 323 BC, a spirit of resistance revived there. A rebellion occurred, spurred on by the oratory of Demosthenes, who had long led Athenian opposition to Macedonia. Antipater, trusted friend of Philip II and Alexander the Great, had been put in charge of Macedonia after Alexander's death. Now he promptly took the offensive and put down the revolt. He demanded that the Athenians hand over the rebels, including Demosthenes. The Athenian assembly condemned them to death. Demosthenes escaped to the island of Calauria, where he took poison rather than surrender.

Noted for his antidemocratic support of the aristocracy, Antipater aroused Athenian opposition further by allowing only citizens who had more than 2,000 drachmas to vote.

The Lamian War: 323–322 BC

The Greek resisters formed the Aetolian League in the mountainous region of Aetolia and an Achaean League around the equally undeveloped Achaea. The leagues fought each other as well as the Macedonians when the occasion arose, but the Greeks never regained their former liberty. Antipater battled the alliance of Greek states in what is called the Lamian War, with little success at first. However, in 322 BC, with the aid of his son-in-law Craters, he once again subdued Greek opposition.

His next battle was with his countryman, the Macedonian general Partakes. Antipater won; Partakes was killed in 321 BC. Antipater was made supreme regent of Macedonia, charged with the care of the children of Alexander. With his death in 319 BC, the regency passed to Polysperchon (who died about 303 BC). Antipater's son Cassander was accorded a minor position but later was made king of Macedonia. Cassander would come into conflict with the diadoch Ptolemy, who was supporting democratic movements in Greece.

Hellenism

Greece entered a period of monarchy and great empires. Macedonia was ruled by the Antigonids, solidly established in their homeland. Outside Macedonia, their position was less strong, but their sphere of influence extended from present-day Bulgaria to the Peloponnisos. The Ptolemies ruled the whole of Egypt, gradually letting go of their possessions outside it. The Seleucid dynasty held the area between the Aegean Sea and an eastern boundary that steadily receded west. Although the diadoch dynasties lived in continual conflict, no single empire achieved dominance. The division of power remained unsettled until Rome stepped in.

The campaigns of Alexander the Great had broadened the international frame of reference of the known world. His career had far-reaching consequences from a political, economic, and social standpoint and initiated a new culture: Hellenism. This concept was not used by contemporaries, but was developed in the nineteenth century to characterize the period between the death of Alexander the Great and the beginning of the Christian era. The term carries chronological as well as cultural implications for scholars, historians, and archaeologists. *Hellenism* is frequently used to refer to the unprecedented spread of Greek culture in the east during

The grand tomb of the Hellenistic king Antiochus I Kommagene (c. 64–38 BC) in Nimrud Dagh (eastern Turkey) is an example of *syncretism* (merging of Greek and eastern art). The large head in the foreground once belonged to a statue of Zeus.

Detail of an Egyptian
relief representing Ptolemy II
Philadelphos. This king
of Greek-Macedonian origin
is depicted as a
traditional pharaoh.

this period. Greek city-states were founded
as far away as Uzbekistan and Kashmir.
These city-states were only small islands of
Greek civilization in an enormous sea of
local cultures—and quite isolated islands, as
well. But Greek was generally used as a *lingua franca* (common language) in large parts
of the Hellenistic empires, without, however,
wholly replacing Aramaic, which had played

When we speak of "Hellenizing," we must take care not to oversimplify the concept. As people and objects became Hellenized in the east, the Greeks themselves spoke of being "Orientalized."

In the new Greek cities, the old gods were not dethroned, but they experienced strong competition from the non-Greek gods, fre-

Two silver coins representing Ptolemy I, king of Egypt (305–283 BC)

quently the Messianic gods whose cults were of an ecstatic nature. Similar Greek cults, especially the Dionysiac religion and mysteries of all kinds, also flourished at this time. Furthermore, the cult of the ruler—the deification of kings—derived strength from the popularity of Messianic gods: The ruler, too, was regarded as a savior or Messiah. Foreign gods were not adopted automatically; they were first adapted to Greek taste. This was done through *syncretism* (detecting similarities between the gods)—for example, between the Egyptian Amon or the Syrian Baal and the Greek Zeus—or by Hellenizing the name and appearance of the foreign deity. The Egyptian goddess Isis became extremely popular.

The Hellenistic era also saw drastic changes on the socioeconomic front. The great stores of Persian gold that were brought into circulation by Alexander and

a similar role in the Persian Empire. Only in areas with a great many Greeks, such as Asia Minor and parts of the Balkans, where Greek culture was encouraged by Hellenistic rulers and, later on, also by the Roman authorities, did it permanently absorb people who were not members of the elite. In most cases, Greeks and the local population existed side by side. Egypt is a striking example.

Marble portrait of Ptolemy I. This is a copy that was made in the first half of the second century BC.

The building of the Olympieion in Athens, a large temple dedicated to Olympian Zeus, that was started in the sixth century BC and taken up again in 175 BC, was only finished in 132 AD.

the diadochs had a powerful inflationary effect. In those days, people had not grasped the fact that a currency can decline in value if the quantity of money increases without corresponding economic growth. Pericles started the Peloponnesian War with 6,000 *talents* (ancient units of weight and money) in the Athenian treasury, which, at the time, was an unimaginably large amount. Under Alexander, such a sum would have been insignificant for the purpose of conducting a major war.

Under Hellenism the newly rich assembled great fortunes by plundering, trade, and banking. Because they actively exploited and invested their capital, they kept a step ahead of inflation. By clever speculation, they could even profit from it. On the other hand, the old landed aristocracy, which was not oriented to a modern money economy, grew rapidly poor. The greatest sufferers were the common people, the leaseholders

and daily workers, for while prices rose, wages lagged behind. Wheat, which had cost five drachmas a bushel in the great days of Demosthenes, almost doubled in price after Alexander. So the masses fell into an ever deeper state of misery. And the specter of indentured servitude arose again for countless unfortunates. Meanwhile, the speculators became richer and richer and lived in unheard-of luxury. Only a few people knew how to profit from the altered conditions.

But there were also reformers who tried to counteract the deteriorating social situation. One example is Cleomenes in Sparta. Even in Sparta, society had become disrupted; nothing remained of the old sobriety. In the city, there were left only 1,000 Spartans with full rights of citizenship, and most of them lived below the minimum required for subsistence. All the wealth was monopolized by a select few. In the last half of the third century, when the situation was ripe for revolu-

Egyptian imitation of a so-called Tanagra statue. During the third century BC, these little statues became very popular in Alexandria as gifts for the dead.

Portrait of
Antiochus I, king of the
Seleucid Empire

Silver coin of
Antiochus IV Epiphanes,
who ruled the Seleucid Empire
from 175-164 BC.
The king is depicted on the
front side of the coin.
On the back is a picture of
Zeus holding Nikè,
the personification of Victory.
The writing reads: "King
Antiochus, the revealed God,
Bearer of Victory."

have arrived, and everywhere in Hellas the oppressed pinned their hopes on Cleomenes, who eagerly stoked the fire of rebellion. This brought him into conflict with mighty Macedonia, which supported the status quo.

Cleomenes was defeated by a coalition. In Sparta, the victors restored the old system, and the king was forced to flee to Alexandria. In the Greek power struggles, the Ptolemies, as we saw earlier, supported popular movements throughout the territory, simply because Macedonia had already formed alliances with the aristocrats. But the spirit of Cleomenes was not dead. Twenty years later, reform-minded groups in Sparta brought the tyrant Nabis to power, and he reinstituted Cleomenes's system, even freeing the slaves. Nabis, however, ran afoul of the Romans, who put an end to his reforms and, to Spartan independence as well.

Greece moved steadily further into a state of crisis. One thing was clear to the Greeks: Nothing could be achieved at home.

Egypt was a specially popular destination for Greek emigrants. The country was at peace, and the kings took a strong interest in its development. For instance, at Fayum in Egypt, hundreds of papyri have been discovered that relate to a land reclamation project. Under the orders of Ptolemy II, Greek engineers had employed an ingenious drainage system there to dry up a lake so that more arable land could be obtained for agriculture. This project and some nearby irrigation systems were implemented under the supervision of the Greek Apollonius, who was also allowed to farm the reclaimed land. He did this partly through slave labor and partly through leaseholders. The land remained the property of the state, and in principle he was supposed to surrender the harvest. Whatever remained from a huge levy, however, he was allowed to sell. Apollonius prospered to such an extent that he was able to open his own weaving mills. Egypt as a whole was exploited in a similar manner. But there, too, it was only a few who profited; the great mass of the population simply grew poorer and poorer as the time went by.

tion, a leader presented himself: Cleomenes, one of the two kings, in power from 235 to 219 BC. After he had managed to defeat a number of Sparta's enemies in war, he returned to his city to bring about a social upheaval. His prestige put him in a position where he could get rid of his opponents and fill the magistracy with his supporters. He then took the radical course of cancelling all debts and divided the land into equal parcels. In addition, several thousand of the *perioikoi* (original inhabitants) were granted full Spartan citizenship. A new era seemed to

Roman copy of a Hellenistic relief from Alexandria. This representation of the three elements, earth, air, and water, is probably an allegory of Egypt. The woman with two children in the middle is the fertile earth. The sea is to the right, and on the left a river is running. The woman who personifies the air is only partly visible on the top left side.

The Greek Legacy

Hellenistic Literature, Science, and Philosophy

In many respects, Greek scholars laid the foundation for modern science and art criticism. From our modern perspective, much of their work seems obvious, but their discoveries were the building blocks for the work of later scientists. Discoveries were made in Hellenic Alexandria, but for the most part, what had been produced there through the previous centuries' scholarship was brought together and passed on for posterity.

The *Mouseion*: Temple of the Muses
The first Ptolemy, Alexandrian astronomer, mathematician, and geographer of the second century AD, gathered a group of scholars at his court. The philosopher Demetrios of

Phaleron arrived from Athens, banished for voting for the losing democrats there. He suggested that Ptolemy establish a center dedicated to the Muses at their temple in Alexandria, a place where one could pursue studies in all the arts and sciences. The Muses, in Greek mythology, were nine goddesses thought to inspire artists of all kinds, including philosophers, poets, and musicians. The daughters of the paramount god Zeus and Mnemosyne, the goddess of memory, each presided over an art or a science. Poetry was so important that it had several Muses: Polyhymnia for sacred poetry, Calliope for epic poetry, Erato for love poetry, and Euterpe for lyric poetry. Terpsichore was in charge of choral singing and dance, Thalia of comedy, and Melpomene of tragedy. Clio presided over history and

Two terra-cotta statuettes of men wrapped in cloaks from the third century BC

A woman wearing a cloak and a sun hat. Terra-cotta statue from Tanagra (Boeotia), made between 300 and 200 BC

Urania over astronomy. Their companions were Apollo, the god of music, and the Graces, the three goddesses of beauty, joy, and charm, who were also daughters of Zeus, this time by the nymph Eurynome. Thalia was associated with good cheer; Aglaia with splendor; and Euphrosyne with mirth.

The Literature of the Museum

Ptolemy thought the center was an excellent idea. The Temple of Muses, called the *Mouseion* (*museum* in Greek) was expanded. Those who were allowed to work there were well-paid servants of the state. They lived at the Museum with their colleagues, overseen by the director and chief priest. It became a true academy of the sciences and literature. Most of its men of letters did not write original creative work. They focused on collecting and preserving traditional styles and works into neatly balanced perfection. The *Iliad* and the *Odyssey*, as we know them, are essentially the work of the Alexandrian scholars. The Museum's archivists collected manuscripts of literary texts like the one attributed to Homer, compared them, and produced new editions. Copies of these were widely sold and greatly prized for their authenticity. The scholars did invaluable work in the area of literary criticism, a discipline that had its start in Alexandria. They provided continuity in ancient traditions with their republishing of the ancient authors and their textual criticism. At the center of the textual criticism was the library of the Museum. It contained an unknown but very large number of scrolls, a unique collection for that time. These texts were literally handwritten, of course; the printing press had not yet been invented.

Writers well versed in language, literary stylistic devices, and mythology were also the sources of new works at the Museum. These can be identified by a certain style characteristic of the Hellenistic poets. One of them, the Greek Theocritus, became famous in the third century BC for his polished poetry. It was a genre that seems to have caught on well. Oppressed by the stench, the noise, and the crowds in Alexandria, people began to idealize life in the countryside. They ascribed an idyllic charm to it, singing its praises in bucolic verse. The Arcadian landscape of Theocritus was filled with amiable shepherds, nymphs, and the sound of melodious music. In the archaic tradition of Arcadia, exemplified by the work of Pausanius, the countryside was rugged and inhabited by bestial divinities and fearsome creatures. Our notion of Arcadia comes from Theocritus by way of the Roman poet Virgil, handed down to the Renaissance period.

Theocritus also wrote comedy, the only genre in which the Hellenistic men of letters were noted for originality. The ancient comedy of Attica was a kind of satirical revue, often political, written for the moment. Among the Alexandrian poets, it was centered around having a tight, structured plot. There is no political satire in what they wrote, nor is there in what is referred to as the New Comedy of Greece. It is characterized instead by stereotypic characters. The great fourth-century BC playwright Menander, for example, told stories of the yearning of a poor girl, the malevolence of a tutor, or the intrigues of a courtesan and a profligate gentleman. Menander was popular in Egypt; his plays have been discovered there on papyrus scrolls. It is no wonder that attempts were made to get him to come to the Museum, but Menander preferred Athens, his city of birth.

The Hellenistic Asclepieion on the island of Kos. This sanctuary for the healing god Asclepios was built in the mid-second century BC.

The Lion of Amphipolis. This statue was probably once a monument for Laomedon, a friend of Alexander the Great. He was the commander of Alexander's naval forces on the Indus, and afterward he became *satrap* (Persian provincial governor) of Syria.

The Exact Sciences

The library in Alexandria was filled with the output of the Museum's scientists as well as literature. The exact sciences also came into their own at Ptolemy's academy. While working there, the Athenian Euclid consolidated the geometry of his time into a very important work, the *Elements*. It is a typical product of Hellenistic science: not an original contribution, but a synthesis of everything that had come before. That does not diminish its importance, however. On the contrary, Euclid's book has had incredible influence and, in some sense, has not been superseded to this day. What is interesting about Greek mathematics is not so much its individual results (for the Egyptians and the Babylonians had already discovered many of them) but its linking of theorems. The Greeks realized that geometry was an integrated system that could be studied through the use of logic.

Mathematics was put to little practical use. Only those with something to construct (temple architects, for example) knew how to use mathematics. Technology was still in its infancy and there was little incentive to develop it. The sheer brute strength of animals and slaves was enough to keep the society going. Another factor in the lack of technology was the haughty attitude usually displayed by the Greek elite, even the intellectual elite, toward practical things. Manual labor, including technology, was considered beneath the level of learned men. Plato, for instance, did not want his beloved geometry to sink to the deplorable level of practical application. In Alexandria, the scientist Hero discovered the principle of the steam turbine. He used it to make an amusing little steam toy to surprise his friends. The technical capability and the materials available at the time precluded any further use.

Archimedes of Syracuse was a great exception to the rule. Whatever mathematical system he discovered he immediately applied. He was very interested in the char-

The so-called Niké of Samothrace (made c. 200 BC). This statue was found in 1863 in the sanctuary of the Great Gods on the island of Samothrace. It is now known as one of the most important statues from the Hellenistic period. The goddess Niké was the goddess of victory, and this statue shows her standing on the prow of a ship in a naval victory.

❮ The so-called Diana (the Roman goddess of the hunt) of Versailles, a Roman copy of a Greek statue of Artemis (the Greek goddess of the hunt) that dates from the fourth century BC

The Greek philosopher Epicurus, who lived between 342 and 270 BC. This statue is a Roman copy of a Greek original that was made around 270 BC.

acteristics of force. It was already known that heavy loads were easier to lift with the help of pulleys and levers, and Archimedes applied his knowledge in this field to everything from slipways to military catapults. "Give me a solid place to stand in space, and I will move the earth," he boasted. He also studied the forces at work in liquids. The result of his research was the following law: a body wholly or partly immersed in a liquid is buoyed up by a force equal to the weight of liquid displaced by that body. This still appears in textbooks as Archimedes's Principle.

Mathematics turned out to be useful in astronomy, as well. The Greeks had observed that the stars remained at approximately the same place in relation to each other throughout the year, except for the moon and the planets Mercury, Venus, Mars, Jupiter, and Saturn. The Greek word *planetes* means wanderer; they gave that name to the celestial bodies they saw "wander." To explain movement, the scholars imagined space as existing in various spheres. They usually assumed the earth as the focal point, thus complicating the calculations. Aristarchus determined that everything was much easier to explain if one conceived of the sun as the central point of the universe and the earth as a component of one of the spheres. He had little success with his concepts. They were too revolutionary for the time.

In the second century AD, Claudius Ptolemaeus suggested a model of the universe centered around a stationary earth. (Called Ptolemy, he was probably born about AD 100 in Greece. The name *Claudius* indicated Roman citizenship and *Ptolemaeus* that he lived in Egypt.) He explained his theory in his first work, writing in Greek. It was translated into Arabic as *al-Majisti* (*Great Work*). In Europe, medieval Latin translations reproduced the title as *Almagesti*, and it has since become known simply as the *Almagest*. Ptolemy used geometry to show that the sun, the moon, and the planets moved in small circular orbits (which he called epicycles) around larger circles, like rings strung on bracelets. To support his contention that the earth was at the center of all these circles, he developed mathematical variations that were accepted until the sixteenth century. They were rejected then by the Polish astronomer Nicolaus Copernicus, who postulated a *heliocentric* (sun-centered) theory that still retained Ptolemy's system of epicycles.

Ptolemy served the Muses well, contributing greatly to several fields of knowledge. He added to the understanding of trigonometry, using it to make sundials and astrolabes to measure the altitude of stars. In *Geography*, he used lines of latitude and longitude to draw maps of the known world. Despite being based on incomplete data, they were used for centuries. He built a device to study light and presented a mathematical theory of the properties of light in *Optics*, known only from its Arabic translation. He offered music theory in *Harmonica*. He used his knowledge of astronomy in the field of astrology, making horoscopes to tell the future in *Tetrabiblos*. Other Alexandrian scholars turned their attention to the shape of the earth. Some insisted the earth was not flat, as generally believed.

The Greek astronomer and mathematician Eratosthenes had already catalogued 675 stars (in a lost work). Now he tried to ascertain the circumference of the earth. He discovered that in two twenty-four-hour periods when day and night were equal, a stick placed vertically in the ground in Syene (now Aswân, Egypt) would cast no shadow at twelve o'clock noon, while a similar stick in Alexandria would cast a shadow one fifth of its length. Using geometry, he calculated the earth's circumference only 3.5 percent off the mark. Eratosthenes, also a geographer and a poet, was made director of the library of Alexandria in 240 BC. He voluntarily starved himself to death about 196 BC, after going blind.

Great advances were made in medical science in third-century BC Alexandria. They were based on the rational approach to medicine of Hippocrates of Kos, called the father of medicine. In his view, disease had natural causes, disassociating medicine from religion and magic. He considered it an art that people could learn, diagnosing disease through an examination of the patient. Born about 460 BC, probably on the island of Kos, Greece, he eventually both practiced and taught medicine there. The seventy works known as the Hippocratic Collection may have actually come from the Kos school of medicine. He is also not likely to have authored the Hippocratic Oath, ethical standards for doctors. He suggested that weather and drinking water can affect the public health, and his method of clinical observation influenced all succeeding generations of doctors. His *Regimen* and *Regimen in Acute Diseases* introduced the concept of preventive medicine through diet and lifestyle.

Herophilus, personal physician to Ptolemy I, is considered the father of human anatomy. Born in Chalcedon (modern Kadikoy, Turkey) about 335 BC, he lived in Alexandria most of his life. Through postmortem dissection, he discovered that the brain is the center of the nervous system and interpreted the separate functions of motor and sensory nerves. He studied the liver, genitalia, eyes, pancreas, and salivary glands. He pioneered research on the blood vessels, learning that they carried blood, not

The *Horologion* of Andronikos of Kyrrhos in Athens, also known as the "Tower of the Winds." This octagonal building, built in the second half of the first century BC, was in use as a water clock (therefore the name *Horologion*). On the outside, the building is decorated with personifications of the winds: on the left we see Notos the south wind, in the middle Euros the southeastern wind, and to the right, Apeliotes the east wind.

air as even Hippocrates had believed. The third-century Erasistratus identified the pumping function of the heart (without understanding circulation). As the century closed, so did an era of intellectual inquiry based on personal observation. Allegiance to dogmas began to play a larger role.

The Skeptics

By the fourth century, the Greek philosophers had spawned a number of schools of thought. The Sophists had found it more important to convince others of their rectitude than to be morally right. Itinerant teachers of philosophy, politics, and rhetoric, they prized skill in clever (if fallacious) argument, providing instruction for a fee. Most of them were Skeptics who denied the possibility of real knowledge of any kind. Plato and his student Aristotle considered them mercenary and objected to their view that truth and morality were matters of opinion. They countered the Sophists' relativism with an elaborate idealism. Plato said the object of knowledge (the idea) had to be fixed, permanent, and unchangeable, based on reason, not sense perception. Reason results in intellectual insight, valid because its object is the eternal substance he called Form. He considered only "the idea" as genuinely real, rejecting the view of empiricism that knowledge (including that based on scientific observation) is based on sense experience.

Skeptics contended that the truth underlying any knowledge is always questionable. Inquiry itself, they held, is a process of doubting. This philosophical school was created by Pyrrho of Elis. The essence of its philosophy was the impossibility of certain knowledge. Pyrrho assumed that man primarily strives for happiness, a balanced life, the sole reason for the practice of philosophy. He said that no human could know the real nature of things; hence, the wise person would suspend judgment. Pyrrho never took sides, believing in observation, *skepsis* in Greek. His followers were called Skeptics. Their questioning of everything, which evolved from the questions and answers of Socrates, gives rise to the modern connotation of the word *skeptic*.

Pyrrho's teachings were a powerful attraction at Plato's Middle Academy in the third century BC and his New Academy of Carneades in the next century. Philosophers at Carneades assumed that knowledge of being was impossible, that no beliefs could be proved conclusively, but that some could be held more probable than others. The norms of morality, they believed, could be understood. While a precise knowledge of the distinction between right and wrong was impossible, it could be approached with a high degree of probability.

Cynicism

Toward the end of the fourth century BC, the eccentric philosopher Diogenes of Sinope

Round altar, found in the *Marmaria*, the sanctuary for the goddess Athena Pronaia in Delphi. It was made in the second half of the second century BC.

The philosopher Chrysippus. The statue is a Roman copy from a Greek original of the third century BC

A depiction of Plato's academy in a Roman mosaic, found in Pompeii. It was made before AD 79, the year in which the city was destroyed in a volcanic eruption.

Painting of athletes
on a Greek vase, made in the
early fifth century BC

Bust of the philosopher
Zeno, who committed suicide
in 262 BC.
The statue is a Roman copy
of a Greek original from
the third century BC.

traveled about the Greek world. Contemptuous of his contemporaries and their values, he was nicknamed *Kyon* (*dog* in Greek), for the odd lifestyle he lived on the fringes of society. Diogenes and his followers were known as *kunikos* (doglike), or Cynics. It is said that Diogenes lived in a barrel and begged his living, considering civilization artificial, based on materialistic interests and unnatural appetites rooted in social convention. He saw the return to a simple, natural life of self-sufficiency and asceticism as the only way to happiness. The wise, he said, should not bother with society, including marriage. His questioning of the sincerity of people's motives has led to today's definition of a cynic as one distrustful of human nature.

Epicurus (341–270 BC)

Epicurus, born and raised on the island of Samos, came into contact with the philosophers of Athens at age eighteen. He established his own school in Mytilene about 311 BC, on the island of Lésvos, leaving it some three years later to direct another school in Lampsacus (modern Lâpseki, Turkey). He settled in Athens in 306 BC, teaching a group of students, both men and women from all over Asia Minor, in the garden of his home. Although the historian Diogenes

Laërtius said in his biography, written in the third century AD, that Epicurus left 300 manuscripts, all but three letters and some fragments have been lost. The Roman authors Seneca, Plutarch, and Cicero all discuss him. In his poem *De Rerum Natura* (*On the Nature of Things*), Lucretius details the doctrines of Epicurus.

Epicurus considered knowledge possible, but only through direct sensory perception. All other knowledge is false unless tested directly against sensory perceptions. His goal was serenity, the freedom from fear of the gods, death, and the afterlife. This was based on his notion of physics, derived from the atomic theories of Democritus and Leucippus. Epicurus considered body and soul alikc to be composed of minute parti-

cles. As the body dissolved at death, so did the soul; no afterlife was possible. The gods had no role to play in this. Epicurus did not deny the existence of gods, but considered them irrelevant to human affairs. He thought them situated in empty space outside the cosmos, too caught up in their own affairs to be bothered with matter. Any fear or veneration of them was as pointless as fear of life after death. Death meant extinction; it had no significance. The goal of life, therefore, was pleasure, and intellectual pleasure was better than sensual, which could disturb one's tranquillity. True happiness could be attained through moderation in sensual pleasure and indifference to it. Prudence, he contended, was a balance between pleasure and pain. He described justice, honesty, and friendship

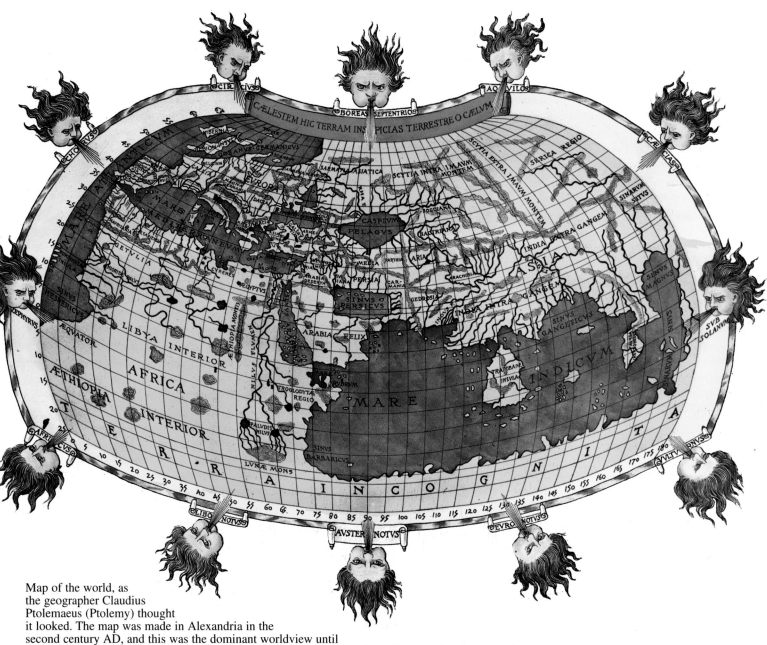

Map of the world, as the geographer Claudius Ptolemaeus (Ptolemy) thought it looked. The map was made in Alexandria in the second century AD, and this was the dominant worldview until the end of the Middle Ages. Australia and the Americas had not yet been discovered and are therefore not on this map, and the Indian Ocean is depicted as an inland sea because people thought that Africa and China were attached to an unknown "south land."

rather than love as virtues. Politics was to be avoided as producing only misery. The wise man has as little to do with society as possible, yet because pleasure is greater when shared, self-interest dictates him to gather a circle of friends around himself.

Relief depicting the fall of Phaëton, the son of Helios, the sun. Phaëton wanted to ride the sun cart although he could not properly control its horses. The result was that the sun came too close to the earth and the earth was in danger of burning. Zeus solved the problem by killing Phaëton with a bolt of lightning.

The Stoic School

About 308 BC, the Cypriot Zeno of Citium established the Stoic school in Athens. The name derives from the *stoa poikile* (painted porch) where he set up the school. He had studied with the Cynic Crates of Thebes and later at Plato's Academy and Aristotle's Lyceum. Two of his disciples, Cleanthes of Assos and Chrysippus of Soli, would carry his philosophy to the known world over the next century, although all of his writings have been lost.

Philosophy, Zeno is supposed to have said, is an orchard. Logic is the gate, physics the ground, and ethics the harvest. His theory was based on the concept that all reality is material, but that matter itself is passive. It is distinct from and acted upon by an active principle, *logos* (word). An eternal force, logos (analogous to god), operated wherever new things came into being. Zeno considered it divine reason, manifested in humans as soul. By living in conformity with nature, one lives in conformity with reason itself and with the universe. He postulated this as a virtue, the only way to attain happiness. All happenings, he contended, are the result of divine will; calm acceptance of them and freedom from passion, grief, and joy was his goal.

Information received through the senses is based on correct perceptions, he said. If mistakes are made, they are due to inaccurate observation and inappropriate processing of the information. The soul that uses reason to digest the information comes to a correct conception of things. Once one has a good conception of virtue, one can then gain virtue. Good was considered to lie in the soul by Stoics as well as Cynics. Good was evident in wisdom and restraint from worldly desires and passions. Drawing from Plato, the Stoics postulated wisdom, courage, justice, and temperance as virtues. One has all of those qualities or none of them. One judges one's action by conscience.

Stoics tried to influence their fellow citizens to act in conformity with nature. They recommended a political career because of the opportunities it offered to practice virtue. There were many Stoics among Rome's notables. The Stoic view that human reason enables the wise to know what nature prescribes led to a theory of natural law that had great impact on Roman jurisprudence. Stoics considered possessions and wealth unimportant in human relationships. They regarded people as naturally equal, manifestations of logos and obligated to help each other. Zeno and his followers rejected many aspects of society they considered irrational, such as the inequality between man and woman or freeman and slave. While competing schools of philosophy were promoting withdrawal from society or the practice of prudent pleasure, the Stoics discussed the brotherhood of humankind and the consequent obligations. On the other hand, they believed that many aspects of society had evolved through reason and were therefore natural. Their success was largely due to the acceptance of the status quo. Stoicism remained the dominant doctrine for centuries, and the Skeptics, Cynics, and Epicureans remained in the minority.

Etruscan bronze depicting Dionysus with two satyrs forming the grip of the so-called *Ficoroni cista* (a *cista* is a box for toiletries). The box was discovered in Praeneste (Palestrina, Italy) and dates from the second half of the fourth century BC.

Ancient Rome

Legendary Founders and Early Kings

While the Greeks were founding their colonies in the eighth and seventh centuries BC, a few huts lay scattered on the hills above the Tiber River on the Italian Peninsula. Farmers, shepherds, and a single merchant had settled amid marshlands along a passable section of the river. Their settlement would be called "Roma." Little is known of Rome's earliest history. What Roman authors recorded much later is a mixture of legend and myth that would become the basis of the shared traditions and national pride of the Roman people.

The Legend of the Founding of Rome

Greek historians of the fifth century BC promoted the myth of Rome's Trojan origin. Rome itself produced no histories until at least 200 BC, with the work of Fabius Pictor. From that point on, the Romans considered themselves the direct descendants of the Trojans. They believed that after the fall of Troy, the hero Aeneas managed to escape with a few faithful to the Tiber estuary where he married a local princess. The great poet Virgil devoted his masterful epic the *Aeneid* to this subject in the first century BC. Aeneas's son Ascanius founded the city Alba Longa just southeast of the modern city of Rome where his successors were to reign for fourteen generations. At that point, the ruling king Numitor was dethroned by his brother

Etruscan tomb from the sixth century BC, that was discovered in Populonia

Picture of the defense wall that, according to Roman tradition, was built by Servius Tullius, one of Rome's earliest kings

Amulius. He arranged for Numitor's daughter, Rea Silvia, to become one of the Vestal Virgins, priestesses forbidden sexual intercourse while they tended the sacred hearth of Vesta. (Originally, two vestals were chosen by the king. Eventually, six were selected by the *pontifex maximus*, the Roman high priest, for thirty years of service, ten each in learning, working, and teaching.)

Nevertheless, Rea Silvia was seduced by Mars, the god of war, and gave birth to twins in the sanctuary of Vesta. Amulius threw the mother in a dungeon and placed the children in a wicker basket on the river. They became stranded in the bulrushes, where they were fed by a she-wolf until a shepherd found them and adopted them. He named the twins Romulus and Remus.

When the brothers had grown, they met old King Numitor who discovered their true descent through a series of coincidences. Together, the brothers began a revolution at Alba Longa. Amulius was killed. The twins, now eager to found their own city, took other pioneers and retreated into the Tiber hills a short distance from Alba Longa. They decided to let the birds decide which of the twins would become king of the new city. It so happened that in Italy a group of priests, known as the *augurs*, interpreted the wishes of the gods from the flight patterns of birds. The practice of consulting an augur before undertaking a major project would continue even much later among the Romans. In this instance, in the confusion stemming from the interpretation, a fight broke out. During it, according to legend, Romulus killed his brother and became the first king of Rome. He would rule until 715 BC.

The future Roman scholar and historian Varro dated the founding of the city to April 21, 753 BC. (Other historians offered different dates.) Romulus determined the city borders by plowing a furrow around it using a bronze plow pulled by a white ox and a white cow. The border demarcated the sacred precinct called the *pomerium* (burial of the dead had to take place outside it). The district included the Palatine Hill, abode of the god Pala. Romulus and his companions danced the whole night through in his honor. This celebration was continued long after Rome was established, in the dances performed during the *Lupercalia* (wolves' feasts) named for the wolves' skins worn by the participating priests.

Rome prospered, but unfortunately the population consisted only of men. To solve this problem, Romulus came up with a ruse. He invited all the neighboring Sabines for a religious celebration just outside Rome. The Sabines eagerly accepted the invitation and brought their daughters along for the ceremonies. At Romulus's signal, every Roman man abducted a Sabine woman. The Sabines tried to win back the kidnapped women in a savage war. During the final battle, however, the Sabine women pleaded with their families to reconcile with the Romans, which they did. The Romans and the Sabines agreed to form one state, jointly ruled by Romulus and the Sabine leader Titus Tatius. According to legend, Romulus did not die, but was taken into the heavens amid thunder and lightning. It was generally believed that Romulus offered his city special protection in the form of the god Quirinus.

After both Romulus and Titus Tatius had passed from the scene about 715 BC, the senate, a council of wise men, elected the elder Numa Pompilius as their successor. He ruled until circa 672 BC. The Romans attributed their religious institutions to this man. He was said to have learned them from a wood nymph with whom he liked to converse. Numa was succeeded in 673 BC by the belligerent Tullus Hostilius who is credited with the destruction of the mother city, Alba Longa, and war against the Sabines.

He was succeeded in 641 BC by the fourth king of Rome, Ancus Marcius or Martius, a grandson of Numa. Ruling until 616 BC, he is famous for a bridge he had built across the Tiber to the Janiculum Hill. A notable conqueror, he seized a number of Latin towns, moving their inhabitants to Rome.

The last three kings of Rome, according to tradition, were Etruscans who represent the influence of Etruria on Rome. According to tradition, they reigned between 616 and 509 BC. The history of the first king is typical of Roman legends. Lucumo was the son of a Corinthian nobleman, Demaratus, who emigrated to the Etruscan city Tarquinii. Lucumo, however, was attracted by what Rome had to offer and moved there with his wife Tanaquil. As they approached Rome, a screaming eagle grabbed the cap from Tanaquil's head. Lucumo interpreted this occurrence as a most favorable omen, and indeed, Lucius Tarquinius Priscus, as the Romans called him, was quick to acquire an excellent reputation. After the death of Ancus Marcius in 616 BC, he was crowned king. Rome prospered during Tarquinius's reign. He had a number of public buildings constructed in the city and his conquests of neighboring peoples added to the population.

Tarquinius Priscus died in 578 BC during a palace revolt and Tanaquil made sure that her husband was replaced by one of her favorites, the head of her household, named Servius Tullius, a man of obscure descent. The Romans honored him as their favorite king and believed they owed their political institutions to him. He had a new constitution drawn up and extended the city borders.

Servius Tullius was murdered in 534 BC by his son-in-law and successor, who was either the son or grandson of Tarquinius Priscus. As king, he was known as Tarquinius Superbus (Tarquin the Proud). History accuses him of the same crimes for which the Greek tyrants are notorious: surrounding himself with a personal guard, pro-

Relief of
two fighting warriors.
Detail of an Etruscan tombstone
from the seventh century BC

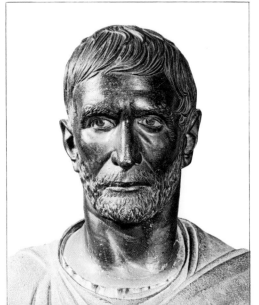

Portrait in bronze of
Lucius Junius Brutus.
He was the leader of the revolt
against the last king of the
Romans, Tarquinius Superbus.
This portrait was made
during the third century BC.

Etruscan wall painting
dating from the
sixth century BC. The mural
was discovered in a tomb
in Tarquinia, named the Tomb
of Hunting and Fishing
after the theme of
this painting.

nouncing judgment at random, and disdaining political institutions. Like most tyrants, he distracted the people with military adventures and monumental construction. It is commonly believed that the city owes its first public sewers, including the great Cloaca Maxima, to Tarquin the Proud. They still function today. He is also famous for having built the temple to Jupiter on Capitoline Hill and having the major streets paved with blocks of granite.

It became increasingly difficult for the Roman people to tolerate oppressive government. In 510 BC, when Tarquin's son Sextus

Vase decorated by a Greek painter called Aristhonothos (his name is on the rim). It dates from c. 650 BC and was found in Caere (Italy). The decoration presents a episode from the *Odyssey*: Odysseus and his friends attacking the Cyclop Polyphemus.

raped Lucretia, the wife of his own kinsman, which led her to commit suicide, the people had had enough. Under the command of Brutus, another distant relative of the king, a revolution broke out. Tarquin was banished, and he and his family escaped. The efforts of Latin cities to reinstall him failed. The people of Rome had decided against having

Example of a so-called Villanova urn from the ninth century BC. The Villanovan people used these urns to bury the ashes after a cremation.

any more dynastic kings. They would henceforth place the power of government in the hands of a *rex* (Latin for king) chosen for life by the council of elders, the first *senatus* (senate).

The True History of Rome:
Life in Latium

Three tribes, the Ramnes, Tities, and Luceres, are mentioned in the legend of Romulus. They are thought to have been the Latin, Sabine, and Etruscan peoples, respectively. Rome is believed to have been conquered by Etruria and ruled by an Etruscan 653 dynasty, probably that of the unpopular Tarquins. Archaeologists and linguists, moreover, reveal another side of Rome's history. They have discovered that the plain between the Tiber and the Apennines was once populated by people who called their land *Latium* and themselves *Latini* or Latins. These inhabitants probably descended from a people who invaded Italy in the course of the second millenium BC. They spoke an

Stone head
representing Mercury,
the Roman god of commerce.
It dates from the end of the
sixth century BC.

Indo-European language and cremated their dead. The oldest settlement that has been excavated dates from the sixteenth century BC. Shortly after 1000 BC, other population groups appeared there who practiced funereal burial. It is not unlikely that they are related to the Sabines of legend. They were also an Indo-European people in Italy who spoke a Latin dialect. Between 900 and 600 BC, many Latin settlements evidently existed on the Tiber hills, each with its own funeral customs. Until the end of the seventh century, Latium remained an underdeveloped rural area. The Latins lived in small villages on the top of hills in huts made of twigs sealed with pitch. The only opening in the hut was a hole in the thatched roof and a door opening in the wall. Urns shaped like these huts were used to hold cremation ashes.

Latium had contact with highly developed cultures, Greek colonies to the south, Etruscans to the north, and sailors from Carthage on its coasts. The area developed quickly at the end of the seventh century. From the politically dominant Etruscans, Latium's major influence, the Latins borrowed technical skills, artistic values, political and religious practices. As the population grew, farmland became scarce and dams and waterworks were built (some of which still exist). The hill villages evolved into *oppida*, small fortified city-states, one of which was Roma. The oppida formed federations, originally only religious in purpose, but eventually political, as well.

Around 625 BC, a city the size of Romulus's pomerium arose in the valley between the Palatine Hill and the Capitoline Hill, made possible by the political unity among the oppida dwellers that occurred when the Etruscans dominated Latium. The word *Roma* is of Etruscan origin.

That Rome was initially ruled by kings is beyond dispute. The Latins had a traditional monarchy. The *rex*, or king, performed the function of supreme judge, high priest, and commander in chief of the army. He led his army personally, following the *lictors*, body guards who carried the *fasces*, the symbol of the *imperium* (royal power). He was advised (upon his request) by the council of elders, or the senate, which also chose a successor. The nomination was accepted or rejected by acclamation in a public meeting or an army assembly. The *populus* (people) were also consulted in matters of war and peace. The monarchy before the Etruscan domination of Rome is thought to have been largely ceremonial. Although the Etruscans gave it greater importance, it gradually disappeared in the oppida of Latium. By 509 BC, the Romans had put an end to both Etruscan power and the monarchy.

Detail of a lid of a
terra-cotta *sarcophagus*
(stone coffin) from Caere
(Cerveteri, Italy).
It dates from
c. 500 BC and represents
a married couple
attending a banquet.

Patricians and Plebeians

Government of the City-state

There were two classes in early Roman society, exclusive of slaves. They were the *patricii* (patricians), who originally had the only political rights, and the other free Romans, the *plebs* (the masses, or plebeians). These people were generally underprivileged peasants and accorded no political rights at first. The class distinction probably originated during the monarchy, but it gained political significance after the last *rex* (king) was deposed.

In Rome, a large share of power was reserved for the heads of families, called the *patres* (fathers; *pater* in the singular). Initially, their authority over their wives, children (whatever their age), and slaves was absolute. Fathers who were interrelated and bore the same family name formed a *gens* (clan). In the beginning, the king ruled the clans through a council of elders, consisting of the fathers of prominent families. Probably the patres who sat on the council began to distinguish themselves from the family heads who did not. The original *senatus*

Wall painting in an Etruscan tomb dating from 530 BC. The Trojan prince Troilus is depicted here on horseback. According to legend, the Trojans moved to Italy after the Trojan War.

(senate) was this council of elders. The patricians comprised the *populus* (people), from which the army was originally drawn. The king called out the populus as needed and led them himself, preceded by his guards (called *lictors*) bearing the *fasces* (bundle), Roman symbol of regal and later magisterial authority consisting of cylindrical bundles of wooden rods, tied tightly together, from which an ax projected. The fasces (the word *fascism* is a derivative) symbolized unity as well as power. Servius Tullius, one of the first seven kings, is usually credited with a major reform that permitted plebeians, who could by then hold property and wealth, to serve in the army. They were assigned rank according to their wealth.

The patrician-plebeian relationship constituted a class struggle, which, to a large extent, charted the course of Rome's domestic history and the development of its governmental organization. Gradually, the social and political barriers against the plebs fell, but for a long time the plebs continued to exist as a separate and unequal class. Marriages between patricians and plebs were not recognized by law, and the children of such marriages lost patrician status.

The patricians formed only a small minority of the free population, however. The fact that they managed to keep power in their own hands for as long as they did was largely due to a very important social institution called the *clientela* (client system). In early Rome, it was customary for free but poor and powerless citizens to bind themselves to a powerful man. Originally, these people, referred to as *clientes*, may have been serfs or tenants of the man in question, but eventually this was not always the case. The *patronus* (patron; one who acted "as a father") could demand obedience and services from his clients. The bond of the clientela, however, was mutual. It was the patron's duty to help clients in case of need (in lawsuits, for example).

Government in the Early Roman Republic

Once the kings were driven out of Rome, the Romans called their state a republic, from the term *res publica* (public thing) or government by the people. (Shortly before the beginning of the Christian era, the state would again fall under the rule of a single person, the Roman emperor. It would then no longer be considered a republic, but a new monarchy called the Roman Empire. The religious functions that the kings once performed were transferred to patrician priests or colleges of priests.

The *Praetors*

Once the regal period ended, with the fall of the Tarquin dynasty, the senate became virtually autonomous. Just as it had previously elected the king for life from the patrician class, it now chose two chief executives to serve on an annual basis. Originally called *praetors* (leaders), they were later given the title *consuls*. At first they were selected exclusively from among the patricians. Neither praetor could overrule the decisions of the other, with the result that neither had the kind of autocratic authority once held by the king. Furthermore, the praetors had no lasting influence, since they were required to resign after a year. The institution of the consulate contributed to making the state an oligarchy, a government run by a few.

The Senate

The controlling minority of the free population comprised the few hundred patricians who ruled the senate and the state. The patres who were already lifetime members confined this membership to their own circle, making it an inherited right, their senate seats passing only to their heirs. Although the last kings may have appointed some plebeians to the senate, the mass of plebs was largely unrepresented in the government until the advent of the republic. Then a second group of senate members was called up: the plebs known as *conscripti* (enrolled). Senators were henceforth called *patres conscripti* (conscript fathers). Although the conscripti also held office for life, they could not pass it on to the next generation.

The *Curiae*

The early Roman Republic also had a popular assembly, the *curiae*, originally made up of clubs (each called a *curia*) of warriors. In

ancient Rome, such clubs confirmed the election of the king. The number of curiae was fixed at thirty, possibly under the Etruscan kings. Their meetings gradually became purely ceremonial, and finally only thirty individuals, in the name of the curiae, officially invested the consuls with their office after their election as the new holders of ruling power. The election itself became the province of another popular assembly.

Mural in the *Tomba dei Auguri* (Tomb of the Auguri) from Tarquinia, ca. 539 BC, presumably representing a priest making a gesture that is associated with mourning

657

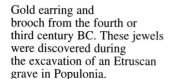

Drawn from the military units called *centuria* (centuries, originally Rome's basic military units), it was called the *comitia centuriata* (committee of centuries).

The *Comitia Centuriata*

During the sixth century, Rome had adopted the Greek mode of warfare, using a phalanx of heavily armed soldiers in close formation, with joined shields and overlapping spears. Service in the Roman army was reserved for people who could afford the requisite expensive military equipment. King Servius Tullius instituted a census to appraise citizen property. Wealth, measured almost exclusively in terms of land, became the criterion for enlistment. Every year a *legio* (military conscription or draft) was drawn from those deemed able to afford military service. Each group of 100 was referred to as a *centuria* (century). From these annual conscriptions, a

Gold earring and brooch from the fourth or third century BC. These jewels were discovered during the excavation of an Etruscan grave in Populonia.

Etruscan vase made of black pottery. It dates from the sixth century BC and was found in Chiusi.

Roman temple of Hercules in Cori, Italy. The temple was built at the end of the second century BC. The bases of these tall columns were originally decorated with red stucco.

new kind of popular assembly developed called the *comitia centuriata.*

It met on the Campus Martius outside the city's sacred *pomerium* (precinct). Men called *juniores* (juniors), drafted between the ages of seventeen and forty-six, made up thirty centuria. Older citizens who no longer went to war did not lose their vote, but made up another thirty centuria, the *seniores* (seniors). These sixty centuria, together with the six centuria of cavalry, formed a propertied class that excluded poorer citizens unable to serve and vote.

The appraisal of citizen landholdings requiring the registration of real estate was accomplished by dividing Rome into *tribus* (districts). Citizens paid *tributum* (tribute or tax) on their land. The army was organized on the same lines, supervised by special officers called *tribunes*. Three tribunes, one for every thousand men, commanded a Roman legion of 3,000 soldiers. The old curiae lost significance as a new popular assembly formed, consisting of the active army and veterans.

By the end of the fifth century BC, the number of Roman citizens had increased. Hence forty, rather than thirty, centuria of juniors were regularly enlisted. The legion also expanded to include less heavily armed citizens who did not need to have as much property in order to serve. The wealthier group were now designated "first class"; the newcomers, "second class." By the third century, there were five separate property classes. In the comitia curiata, the first class (ultimately made up of eighty centuria) consisted of juniors and seniors. It was now joined by four lower classes, making a total of ninety centuria. Four additional centuria were reserved for army specialists. All remaining citizens who were too poor to serve except as light-armed soldiers were grouped into a single centurium. During this period the cavalry had also swelled to eighteen, which usually voted with the centuria of the first class. Thus, the first class predominated, ninety-eight centuries to ninety-five. At the same time, the number of districts outside the city of Rome had increased to thirty-one, as a result of the Roman conquests in Italy. In the middle of the third century BC, the final reform took place, establishing an intricate relationship between the five classes of property and the total of

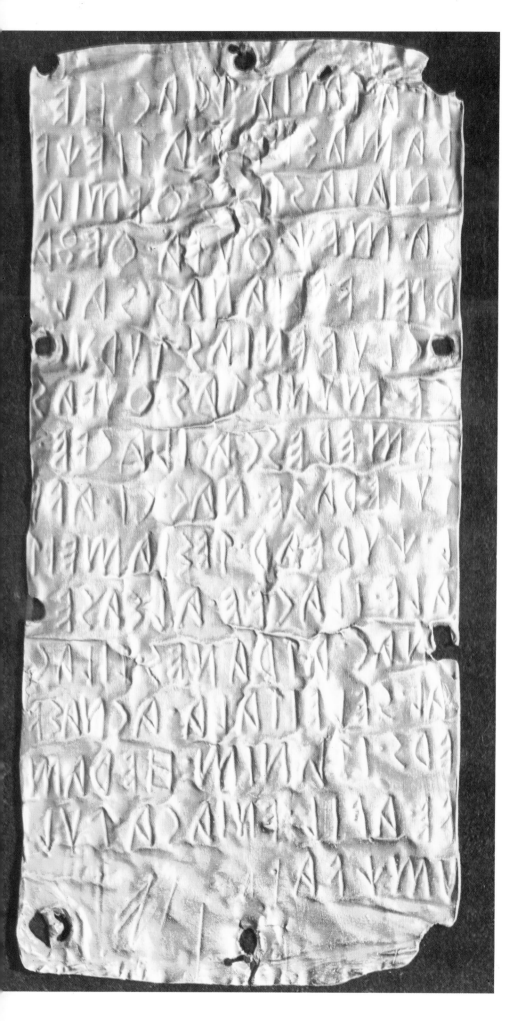

thirty-five districts. As a consequence, the first class was reduced from eighty centuria to seventy. Through an alliance with part of the second class, the wealthier strata of Roman society continued to hold a majority in the assembly. It had not adopted a "one man one vote" rule, but instead voted by centuria.

New Institutions in the Roman Class Struggle

The Roman class called plebs was never a homogenous social phenomenon, either economically or culturally. There were poor plebs, middle-class plebs, and even, to an increasing degree, wealthy plebs. The poorest sought only a piece of land and the revocation of the strict debt law which could have a debtor sold into slavery. The richest plebs had political ambitions. They wanted a share of the power and the privileges of the patricians. Many of the most respectable plebs had come from places outside the city that had been conquered by Rome. They had held prominent positions at home and, after moving to Rome, wanted comparable status. In this case, class struggle was closely related to the expansion of the Roman Republic.

The *Tribuni Plebis*

In 494 BC, most of the plebeian soldiers threatened to secede from Rome. According to legend, they withdrew to a nearby mountain, formed an assembly called the *concilium plebis* (council of plebs), and threatened to found a separate city if the patricians refused to recognize their assembly and the officials it chose. These officials were called *tribuni plebis* (tribunes of the plebs; by extension, of the people). Eventually, ten tribunes were chosen to protect the interests of the plebs. They could intervene if a plebeian were in danger of being punished unjustly. They could override decisions of the magistrates by speaking the single word *veto* (I forbid). The tribune was declared inviolable by the plebeians. The concilium plebis vowed to the gods that anyone harming a tribune could be killed.

The *Decemvirate*

One Roman milestone was the establishment of a special commission of ten learned men known as *decemvirs* (ten men) in 450 BC. The task of the Decemvirate was to record

A gold tablet
(c. 500 BC) from Pyrgi,
the harbor of Caere.
The Etruscan text describes a
dedication to the goddess
Uni by Thefarie Velianas, the
ruler of Cisra.

all common law. The resulting compilation was known as the Laws of the Twelve Tables because the laws were engraved on twelve bronze tablets that were placed in the Roman Forum. From that point on, the patrician magistrates could no longer make legal decisions wholly at their own whim, but instead measured their judgments against this formal standard. In theory, the tables granted equality of rights to all free citizens. In practice, however, the weak and the vulnerable still had to rely on powerful patrons for protection or legal redress. The right of appeal to the popular assembly may well have been established at this time.

The Canuleian Law

In 445 BC, the plebeians won another important victory, when the prohibition on marriages between patricians and plebeians was repealed. Intermarriage was declared legal by the Canuleian Law. Rich plebeian families could now enter into alliances with patricians, a change that was bound to have long-range political consequences.

The *Comitia Tributa*

By the middle of the fifth century, a new popular assembly of the *comitia tributa* (assembly of the districts; by extension, of the people) was formed. The assembly of the comitia tributa was set up on the model of the concilium plebis, but it was an assembly of all classes of Roman citizens, plebeians and patricians. Votes were taken by tribes or districts, just as they were taken by centuria in the comitia curiata. However, no distinc-

Etruscan urn (box for keeping ashes). The figure on the lid represents the deceased. The box was made in the first or second century BC in Volterra.

tion in terms of wealth was recognized. Within each district, the principle of "one man one vote" was acknowledged.

Rome had grown too large to be governed by only two officials. For some time the consuls had been appointing assistants, called *quaestores*, to handle the lower level of criminal cases. Eventually they were chosen by the comitia tributa. Shortly after that, two additional quaestors were put in charge of public finances. The quaestors had now become magistrates, chosen each year by the people. From its inception, plebs were permitted to be elected to this office.

Picture of a dancer. This mural was discovered in the Etruscan tomb of the *triclinium*, or dining room, in Tarquinia (470 BC).

661

The *Aediles*

As early as the fifth century, the position of *aedile* (temple functionary) was established, another official magistracy to which plebeians could be elected. There were originally two aediles, connected with an important plebeian cult center, a temple on the

Small bronze statue
of an Etruscan warrior
from the
fifth century BC

The Laws of the Twelve Tables

The plebeians began their resistance to patrician rule with fierce demands for written laws. They hoped to put an end to the arbitrary practices of the patrician upper class. In 451 BC, under the pressure of these demands, the patricians appointed a Committee of Ten (the *Decemviri*), who were given the task of setting down the common law of Rome in clear, equitable terms. There is little information about the Decemviri. Most of the Roman sources contradict one another. It is not known how they were appointed or for how long, but it is certain that they were all patricians.

Their work was known as the Laws of the Twelve Tables, because the laws were engraved on twelve bronze tablets that were placed in the Roman Forum. They reflect the patriarchal control of the agrarian Roman society in which they were written, based as they were on the powerful family bonds and the almost unlimited authority of the *pater familias* (father of the family). He had the power of life and death over his wife and children (except for newborns), his slaves, and his plebeian clients, though he was obliged to call a family council before making a life-and-death decision. The position of the woman in society was completely subordinate to that of the man. Upon marriage, she exchanged the authority of her father for that of her husband. If he died before her, she was put in the custody of a male relative.

Crimes against private property were severely punished. A person whose property had been stolen had the right to put the thief to death. Agriculture was given special protection. A person who maliciously set fire to another's crops or tried to destroy them could be burned alive. Regulations on loans and leases were very strict. A debtor who could not pay his debts was regarded as a criminal. His creditor could put him to death

or sell him as a slave outside Roman borders. If there was more than one creditor, the debtor could be cut into pieces!

These laws reflect the society's predominant interest in possessions. Other provisions seem more enlightened. It was provided, for example, that marriage could be ended by mutual consent. If a wife remained absent from the marital bed for three nights and declared herself unwilling to return, the marriage could be dissolved. The father was obliged to give his sons (but not his daughters) a good education. The right to form associations for commercial purposes was

established. The Twelve Tables contain almost no legislation with regard to politics, but they did provide for the right to appeal decisions of a judge, requiring that the appeal be submitted at the popular assembly. Providing a foretaste of Latin as the language of jurists and administrators, these laws were never abolished.

Bronze statue dating from 400 BC representing a farmer with two plow oxen. It was discovered in Arezzo.

Etruscan bronze statue representing Minerva, the goddess of wisdom and knowledge

Aventine Hill dedicated to the triad Ceres (the goddess of agriculture) and Liber and Libera, a pair of fertility and cultivation deities. As state officials, the aediles were in charge of public works, the public food supply, and the markets.

The number of magistracies that could be occupied by plebs steadily increased. As a result, more and more plebeians came to be in the senate. But the most important post and the one most coveted by prominent plebs, that of the consul, the highest magistrate, remained in the hands of the patricians.

The Licinian-Sextian Laws

In 367 BC, the power finally shifted. A bill was presented in the comitia tributa by two tribunes, Licinius and Sextius. The following year the first two magistrates known as consuls consisted of a plebeian and a patrician. It was not long before a new law decreed that pairing must take place. In 366 BC, Sextius became the first plebeian consul. The same year, yet another new official appeared: the *praetor*. (The former consul-praetors were now known simply as consuls.) The praetor was primarily concerned with the administration of justice, but he could also command an army. Like the consuls, the praetor was elected by the comitia centuriata, the old military assembly, but he was a colleague of lower rank. (In 337 BC, the first plebeian would be elected to this office.) In 356 BC, the first plebeian was appointed to the unusual post of dictator. The concept of dictatorship had been taken over by the Romans from the Latin League in the fifth century BC. At that time it was a military command lasting for six months and only granted in case of exceptional need or great danger. During that time period everyone was subject to the authority of the dictator, whose power automatically came to an end.

Finally, in 351 BC, a plebeian was elected

Bronze brooch dating from the third century BC. The picture represents Mithras killing the bull. Mithras was originally a Persian sun god, whose cult came to Italy, probably during the first century AD. The cult was only accessible to male worshipers. Because Mithras was associated with victory, he became very popular with soldiers throughout the Roman Empire.

Roman limestone relief dating from the third century BC. The relief represents Hades, the god of the underworld, and his wife Persephone. The Danaids, the fifty daughters of King Danaus of Argos stand behind them. These women (all except one) murdered their husbands on their wedding night and were condemned in the underworld to carry water in sieves.

The Via d'Abbondanza in Pompeii. The houses date from the third and second century BC and were two stories high.

as a *censor* for the first time. This was a relatively new office, to which two men were elected every five years. The censors were responsible for conducting the census and registering new members in the senate. If necessary, they could also expel unworthy members from it, making the office one of strong moral significance and great prestige.

The empowerment of the plebeian brought about a rapid change in the composition of the senate, which, by the end of the fourth century, was predominantly plebeian. The composition of the senate improved its relationship with that purely plebeian assembly, the concilium plebis. This body elected the tribunes of the people and passed resolutions that officially related only to the plebs, but that in practice affected everyone.

The End of the Class Struggle

In 287 BC a historic law was enacted, the *lex Hortensia*, named after the plebeian dictator Hortensius. It provided that a decree of the plebeian assembly should have the same effect as a decree or *lex* (law) of either of the two other assemblies, the comitia centuriata or the comitia tributa. This changed the class struggle. The upper stratum of the plebs had achieved their goal. The poorer plebs also had cause for satisfaction since, over the course of the fourth century, the cruel debt law had been modified. No debtor could be sold any longer as a slave, and land was now regularly distributed among the less well-to-do Romans.

A new elite now emerged in Roman society, the *nobiles* (nobles), a mixture of plebeians and patricians who had held the highest office (the consulate), or whose fathers or forefathers had done so. This new hereditary ruling class of *nobilitas* (nobility) controlled the senate and, thanks to their array of clients and their own prestige, the popular assemblies as well. Once accorded little actual administrative authority, the senators now dominated government in both domestic and foreign affairs.

Senatorial power had increased with the power of Rome, the patrician-plebeian struggle was over, but Rome never became a democracy, even after the emancipation of the plebs. The year 287 BC did mark the beginning of a period of relatively harmonious cooperation among the highest circles of Roman society, but had little effect on the lowest segment of society, the poor plebs. Although there was comparative peace on the Italian Peninsula and unparalleled expansion abroad, the old class contest would reemerge in the political arena as the aristocratic and the popular parties fought for control.

666   Roman marble relief from the second century BC depicting a butcher at work in his shop

Two soldiers carrying a dead comrade form the handle on the lid of an Etruscan *cista* (case in which toiletries were kept), that was found in Palestrina, fourth century BC.

From City to State

Rome Conquers the Italian Peninsula

Initially, Rome was one of many hundreds of small city-states on the Italian Peninsula. It lay between the territories held by Latium and Etruria, and both Latins and Etruscans fought hard over the city.

The rise of Rome seems to have begun with the struggle of the Latin Alliance against the Etruscans. It is possible that no city felt the Etruscan influence quite as strongly as Rome. During the sixth century, the Etruscans ruled the territory between the valley of the Po River and Campania while,

in the south, its influence reached to the Greek colony at Cumae and the Bay of Neapolis (Naples). The Greeks of the southern Italian Peninsula were always on a war footing with the Etruscans (or Thyrrenoi, as they called them). To meet the Thyrrenoi at sea was the nightmare of every Greek sea captain. In about 535 BC, the Etruscans allied themselves with the powerful Carthaginians across the Mediterranean Sea in order to dislodge the Greeks from the establishment of Alalia, on the island of Corsica.

Fifty years later the tide turned when a massive attack on Greek Cumae failed. A few years later, the Latin Alliance rebelled. Near Aricia just south of Rome, the alliance defeated the Etruscans with the help of Cumae. The allies established a shrine to Diana, favored goddess of the Romans, in Aricia. Aricia became the predominant power within the alliance, leading the battle to force the Etruscans out of Latium. Their last major attack (in 474 BC), near Cumae, was repelled by forces led by Greece.

Rome remained a contested area for quite some time. An echo of these crucial wars is found in the legends surrounding Lars Porsenna, an Etruscan ruler who, according to tradition, attempted to return the Tarquins to power. The Romans reputedly demon-strated great courage in the wars that followed. This was exemplified by Horatius Cocles, who singlehandedly held back the Etruscans while his comrades behind him pulled down a strategic bridge and survived to tell the tale. Another story is that of Mucius Scaevola, who was captured when he tried to kill Porsenna. Without a grimace he placed his hand on hot coals to show that torturing him would get the Etruscans nowhere and that the people would resist if the war continued.

Porsenna dominated Rome for some time to come and, although he never occupied the city, the Roman Senate gave him an ivory throne and staff, a golden crown, and a royal purple robe.

Rome acquired *hegemony* (domination) in the Latin Alliance early in the fifth century. In about 493 BC it defeated a Latin army near Lake Regillus. At last Rome was strong enough to take the offensive alone against the Etruscans. About 400 BC the Romans took the wealthy city of Veii, twelve miles (twenty kilometers) northeast of Rome on the Etruscan side of the Tiber. They demolished the city and cast its inhabitants onto the slave market.

Threat of the Gauls

Around 400 BC a series of tribes streamed across Central Europe to the west. They called themselves Celts or Gauls and spoke a language heavy with consonants. Remnants of this language are used today in Wales, Ireland, Scotland, and Brittany. Some Gallic groups penetrated deep into the territory of Mediterranean civilizations.

Several years after the Roman conquest of Veii, a troupe of Gauls showed up in Etruria, where the city of Clusium asked Rome to come to its aid. Rome thus acquired a new opponent. It thought these barbarians could be easily destroyed, but at the Allia River north of Rome a Latin-Roman army was nearly annihilated. The defeat was so complete that the Romans gave up the city and sought safety in flight all over Latium. Only the Capitoline Hill, with its temple and its fortress, was capable of defense. From that high ground the defenders watched and prepared themselves for siege as the Gauls burned their city to the ground.

Many legends arose around the siege of the Capitoline. The eldest senators reputedly refused to vacate the city. Together, dressed in their official robes, they waited for the Gauls and together they were slain. When the Gauls tried to take the hill garrison by surprise, through a badly guarded entrance, it is said that the sacred geese in the temple warned the Romans with their honking. It is

Etruscan ornament, made of forged gold and found in Caere

Urn shaped as a little house, in which the ashes of the deceased were kept. It was found in the *necropolis* (city for the dead) of Villanova, eighth century BC

668

Top of the lid of an Etruscan bronze urn that was excavated in Capua. It depicts a satyr abducting a *maenad* (madwoman).

not certain whether the Capitoline was spared. The Gauls, warring primarily to gain booty, were finally bought off with a tribute of 1,000 (375 kilograms) pounds of gold. The story goes that the Romans complained about the way in which the gold was being weighed. In reply, Brennus, the Gallic leader, immediately added his gigantic sword to the weights on the scale. "*Vae victis*," he is supposed to have said. "Woe to the vanquished." In the end the Gauls only settled in what is now the northern Italian Peninsula, an area the Romans did not consider a part of the Italian Peninsula proper. They called it *Gallia Cisalpina* (Gaul on this side of the Alps) to distinguish it from *Gallia Transalpina* (Gaul across the Alps).

Ally Becomes Ruler

Rome held the predominant power within the Latin Alliance. In matters of foreign pol-

icy, there was no doubt that Rome had the decisive voice. But the Romans continued to gather ever more influence. Latium was surrounded by infertile mountain areas. The inhabitants of these regions would often descend to conquer land in the plains. In the struggle against these intruders, Rome's prestige grew with every victory, resulting in envy and uneasiness among its subordinates. The Latins became increasingly convinced that Diana's shrine had stood on Aventine Hill long enough. In 358 BC the most impor-

Heavily armed Samnite soldier. The Romans fought the Samnites in the process of expanding their empire over the entire Italian Peninsula.

tant Latin cities challenged Rome. With the assistance of the rest of the Latins, Rome managed to ward off the threat. Ultimately, all the Latins had to accept a much tighter alliance. By this time, Rome was ruler.

Rome's position is illustrated in its treaty with Carthage in 348 BC. "The Romans and their allies," the Greek Polybius copied two hundred years later from the state archives, "shall not sail beyond Cape Fariria, except when they feel obliged in case of storms or enemies. If they enter our [Carthaginian] harbors, they shall not buy or take anything, except what is necessary to repair their ships and to bring sacrifices to the gods, and they shall leave within five days. The Roman ships entering harbors to trade on the coast of Africa or Sardinia shall not have to pay any taxes, except the salaries of the town crier and the administrator, and with all sales that are accomplished with the help of these officials the state will guarantee payment to the seller. And the same holds when any Roman ship enters a harbor in the part of Sicily dominated by the Carthaginians. At the same time, the Carthaginians promise to respect those Latin cities that are subject to Rome, and even those other Latin cities not immediately dependent on Rome. In case the Carthaginians feel obliged to occupy one of these cities, they promise to restore them without any costs to the Romans and under no condition will they build any fortification on Latin territory. If Carthaginians enter Latium under arms, they shall not be allowed to remain there beyond sundown."

Rome thus clearly acted as ruler of Latium, and the Latins had few reasons to be satisfied with the new ruler. During a war with the Samnites, an alliance of mountain tribes from the southern Apennines, tribal interests were obviously sacrificed in favor of Rome's. Immediately after that war, the whole league rebelled. The battles continued for two years. The Latins were on the defensive from the start because the Samnites were allied with Rome. In 338 BC final resistance was broken. The Latin League was abolished, a number of cities were made part of Rome, and all other cities were forced to enter into a separate league.

Remains of the Roman road that connected Rome with the Etruscan city of Vetulonia. The system of Roman roads remained the most important traffic network in Europe until the Middle Ages.

Bust of Pyrrhus, the king of Epirus, who tried to create a large realm as a dictator. The Romans did not accept these military incursions into their territory, however, and after 275 BC Pyrrhus's attempts came to an end.

The Struggle against the Samnites

The Samnites did not remain allies of Rome for very long; in the end, their interests opposed those of the valley dwellers. For decades the Romans carried on bloody wars against the alliance of warlike tribes, suffering several heavy defeats. Rome had to fight the Samnites, who had already conquered several Greek territories, for the first time in 343–341 BC when the Latin Alliance was still in existence. Capua offered itself to Rome in exchange for protection when it found itself threatened. Rome accepted, initiating its involvement with the southern part of the Italian Peninsula. One by one the cities to the south of Capua fell to Rome. The city-state consolidated its power by establishing

colonies, small settlements inhabited by able-bodied civilians mostly drawn from the Roman proletariat.

The longest war between Rome and the Samnites raged from 327 to 304 BC. In 321 BC the consuls went on an offensive campaign, entering Samnite territory with their armies. Surrounded by Samnite warriors at Caudine Forks, they were forced to capitulate after a few days of fighting. They were allowed to retreat, but the Samnites subjected consuls, officers, and soldiers to the humiliation of "passing under the yoke," a low gateway of lances. The captured consuls

Etruscan terra-cotta statue of two winged horses that was found in Tarquinia. It was made in the fourth century BC.

Etruscan fresco with
a battle scene found in the
so-called Tomb of the
Amazon in Tarquinia.
It dates from the
fourth century BC.

had to sign a peace treaty. It was rejected by the senate, and war continued. Another consul was defeated by the Samnites in 309 BC. The Romans changed tactics; avoiding aggression, they awaited attack by the mountain tribes. It came in 305 BC, with a Samnite invasion of Campania. This time the Romans won. A year later, they made peace with the Samnites, putting Campania under permanent Roman control. Hostilities resumed in 298 BC. It took the Romans until 290 BC to eliminate the last of the Samnites in one last great war. Only the Greek colonies in the south of the Italian Peninsula remained independent of Rome.

Pyrrhus and His Victories

The Greek colonies could have been the most dangerous enemies of Rome had they acted in unison and, especially, had they received assistance from their mother city-

states in Greece. By the time Rome defeated the Samnites, these cities had long since severed all contacts with their colonies in the Italian Peninsula, forcing them to hire mercenary generals (usually from Greece) to command their armies.

Rome became involved in the affairs of Greece because the Athenian colony of Thurii sought its support against the Lucanians. Soon other Greek cities placed themselves under Rome's protection. This alarmed Tarentum, the most powerful Greek city on the Italian Peninsula. The inhabitants of Tarentum considered the Romans barbarians, whose improper meddling into their affairs deserved punishment. After some initial skirmishes, they realized the strength of their opponent and proceeded to hire a Greek general. Their choice was Pyrrhus, king of Epirus, a kingdom located on the Greek coast across from the heel of the Italian boot.

Pyrrhus was an extremely ambitious man who dreamed of creating a large empire. He gladly seized this opportunity. He raised a disciplined army that included twenty elephants and set himself up as dictator in Tarentum. He ordered the theaters and gymnasia closed and forced civilians to eat military fare and to engage in military exercises. This did not make him popular. The Romans fought hard against Pyrrhus, yet he managed twice to emerge victorious: at Heraclea in 280 BC and at Asculum in 279 BC. Both times, however, the Romans offered fierce resistance and the Greeks suffered enormous losses. "One more victory like that and I will be lost!" Pyrrhus is reputed to have exclaimed. A victory so costly as to be tantamount to defeat has since been called a "Pyrrhic victory."

Legend has it that at one point when the senators seemed ready to give in to Pyrrhus, the former censor Appius Claudius, paralyzed and blind, was brought into the senate in a sedan chair. He told the assembly that he never had reconciled himself to being blind, but that he now would prefer to be deaf as well, so as not to hear of the disgraceful treaty Rome was about to conclude. The senate was deeply impressed with his words and the treaty talks with Pyrrhus were called off. As late as Cicero's time (second half of the first century BC), the text of Claudius's speech was considered a masterpiece of eloquence.

Etruscan bronze mirror, made in Palestrina at the end of the fourth century BC

673

After his two victories, Pyrrhus believed that the Greeks of the southern Italian Peninsula could manage for themselves. He went to try his luck in Sicily, where he scored great victories against the Carthaginians. Meanwhile, the Romans drove the Tarentans into a corner once again. Pyrrhus crossed over to the Italian Peninsula yet another time to relieve his *protégés*. In 275 BC his army met the Romans near the city of Malventum, near Campania, but now his troops were no match for the stronger

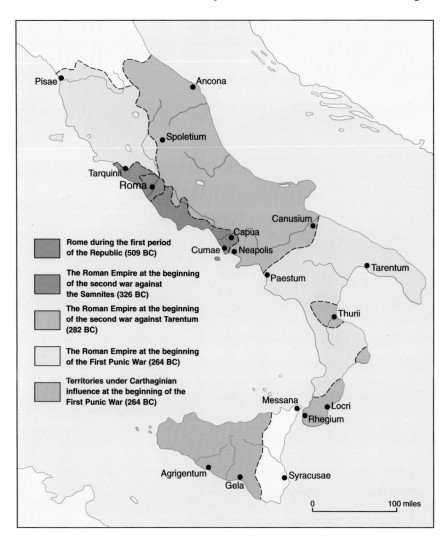

Rome during the first period of the Republic (509 BC)

The Roman Empire at the beginning of the second war against the Samnites (326 BC)

The Roman Empire at the beginning of the second war against Tarentum (282 BC)

The Roman Empire at the beginning of the First Punic War (264 BC)

Territories under Carthaginian influence at the beginning of the First Punic War (264 BC)

0   100 miles

Roman conquests
in Italy (500–264 BC)

Romans. It is said that they routed Pyrrhus's elephants with burning arrows, thus turning the tide of battle. Three years later Tarentum was forced to recognize Rome's superiority. By then Pyrrhus was back home. He died on a campaign in Greece when a woman dropped a roofing tile on his head in the city of Argos. The Romans thought that Malventum sounded rather like *maleventum* (bad wind). They renamed it *Beneventum* (good wind) after the Roman victory.

The Roman Army
By 270 BC, all of the Italian Peninsula south of the River Po was subject to Rome, the

The Etruscans

Etruscan
bronze statue
of a soldier,
made in the fifth
century BC

674

The origin of the Etruscan people is unclear, largely because little is known about their language. To this day their inscribed texts have not been deciphered. Two theories about their origin enjoy some degree of support. The first holds that they originated somewhere in Asia Minor, in the region of Lydia or the Aegean Sea, before the time of the Greeks. The basis for this stems from a statement by the Greek historian Herodotus and an inscription on the isle of Lemnos in a language bearing close resemblance to Etruscan. The second theory considers the Etruscans the descendants of the *autochthonous* (earliest known) population of north and middle Italy, bearers of the so-called Terramare and Villanova cultures.

The first theory may be somewhat more likely. Herodotus and the Greeks called the Etruscans the "Tyrrhenoi." Egyptian inscriptions from the thirteenth century BC also list the "Tursha" among several seafaring peoples. The name could refer to the Greek *Tyrrhenoi* or Tyrsenoi. Certain religious rites of the Etruscans, such as the observation of the liver of sacrificial animals in divination and prophecy bear strong resemblance to Babylonian customs that also penetrated Asia Minor. The mounting and arrangement of many Etruscan graves are similar to those found in Asia Minor. The Etruscans are said to have come to the Italian Peninsula in successive waves, where they met the Villanova culture, which was already engaged in mining. The Etruscans brought with them a highly developed culture, previously open to contact with the Greeks. The Etruscans adopted the Greek alphabet in the seventh century BC, as well as many Greek myths and legends. They sought Greek arts and crafts and bought painted Greek vases as early as the late eighth century BC. Etruscan potters and painters soon began imitating Greek ceramics.

The Etruscans were organized in city-states originally ruled by kings, but in the fifth century BC the kings were replaced almost everywhere by aristocracies (as was the case in Rome). The cities united in a loose federation with a common sanctuary, but without a political center. The pre-Etruscan population had been subjected to servitude, but part of it was probably absorbed into the upper layer of Etruscan society. The presence of iron, copper, and silver mines contributed considerably to the prosperity of Etruscan cities and their elites, as did the export of bronze objects and ceramics. Well into the fourth century BC, Etruscan sailors were esteemed as traders and notorious as pirates in the Mediterranean. They generally worked with

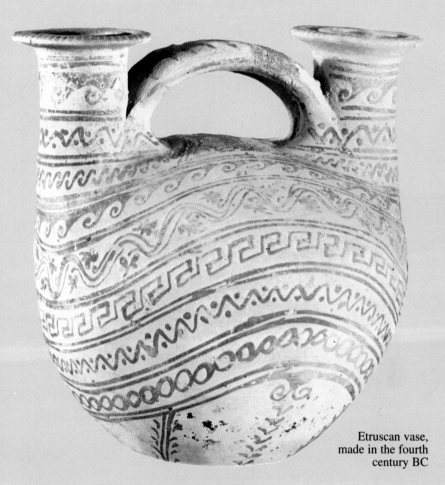

Etruscan vase, made in the fourth century BC

the Carthaginians against Greek competitors.

The height of the Etruscan political power came in the sixth and fifth centuries BC, declining thereafter under the frequent attacks of Greeks, Latins (and Romans), and Gauls. But their exquisite mural painting flourished in rich tombs (such as those preserved today at Tarquinia) as late as the third century BC. After their territory, roughly the size of modern Tuscany, had been seized by the Romans, their language gradually disappeared. They were ultimately absorbed into the culture of Roman Italy.

Detail of a vase,
painted with pictures of
soldiers in full battle.
It dates from the fourth
century BC.

result of many wars, not all successful by any means. Nevertheless, Rome had always carried on the struggle, renewing it even after defeat. It constantly improved its armament, tactics, and organization, and always adapted to a certain degree to its opponents. As the Roman state expanded, it sometimes exterminated or enslaved conquered cities and peoples. But more often than not, they were incorporated into Roman territory, sometimes at once, sometimes after a few generations. The number of Roman civilians and soldiers grew steadily, as did the number of allies throughout the Italian Peninsula.

Gradually, Rome reached a point where its numerical supremacy alone assured victory in any war, no matter how many battle defeats it suffered. War on the Italian Peninsula was a common phenomenon, used primarily to acquire and retain territory. A militaristic mentality dominated most of the inhabitants, above all the Romans. Beginning with ancient Rome, the aristocracy always sought fame and prestige, which meant military fame and military prestige. The Roman noble was always ready to go to war, and the masses were only too eager to follow. Successful wars meant conquest and new allotments of land.

The Porto all'Arco, ❯
an Etruscan gate that is still
in use in Volterra,
the capital of northern
Etruria

677

The Roman *legio* (legion) of the early fifth century BC consisted of 3,000 heavily armed troops. It increased to 6,000 heavy infantry troops and 2,400 light infantrymen over the fourth century BC. In 366 BC the annual draft was split between the two consuls, each commanding a legion of 4,200 men. During the great war with the Samnites, this annual army was doubled to four legions, two for each consul, in proportion to the growth of Rome's population. The legion still maintained several lines of heavily and less heavily armed soldiers. This reflected the various property classes in the civilian population. By the third century BC, the armament became generally uniform. It consisted of a bronze helmet, a *scutum* (large leather covered shield), two javelins, and a sword. Richer soldiers also had a metal *cuirass*, a piece of armor covering the back and chest.

The Romans borrowed the organizing principle of *maniples* (three lines of ten) from the Samnites, resulting in greater flexibility on the battlefield. Rome's allies provided about as many separate troops to the state armies as the Romans did themselves. They, too, were organized in maniples and legions, but they were commanded by Roman officers. Since the conquest of Veii, the soldiers received a modest salary from the public treasury. The sons of senators and of a growing group of rich civilians who were not senators served in the cavalry, 200 to 300 men in each legion. The army was very well disciplined. The consuls, who generally acted as supreme commanders, held power over the life and death of their troops and did not hesitate to use it to reinforce command.

Most conquered cities and peoples on the Italian Peninsula retained local autonomy. When a state had been defeated, those in power were generally required to cede part of their territory to Rome. The land was then divided among rich and poor alike. Sometimes Rome established a military colony of able-bodied men to keep watch over a given region. Such men were exempt from campaign duty.

Treaties were signed with the conquered that gave both parties equal rights in most matters except the political. The Latins were the people most closely allied to Rome. Latin men were even allowed to vote in the *comitia tributa* (assembly of the people) if they happened to be in Rome. Other communities, unable to exercise any influence in the political field, nevertheless enjoyed complete Roman citizenship in the private sphere. Together the cities that had such rights were called *municipia* (municipalities). Their inhabitants possessed all the duties and obligations but not all the rights of Roman citizens. The Romans never spoke of such people as subjects. They were termed *socii* (allies) and were thought of as sharing the interests of Rome.

Detail of an Etruscan wall painting, depicting a funeral scene. This was made in the fourth century BC and was found in a tomb in Tarquinia.

Bronze liver that was used for predicting the future. The forecaster compared this model with the liver of a sacrificial animal and then explained the meaning of the differences.

The Carthaginian general Hannibal used elephants in the war against the Romans. The elephants were supposed to frighten the Roman foot soldiers, but needed a lot of care. They were therefore soon abolished as war matériel. Terra-cotta statuette from the Hellenistic period

Duel for the West

The Punic Wars

Carthage and Rome Battle over Sicily: Third Century BC

Its victory over Tarentum and its general Pyrrhus in 275 BC left Rome, with its allies on the Italian Peninsula, one of two great powers in the western Mediterranean. The other was Carthage, on the northern coast of Africa, with its subject areas in North Africa, Sardinia, and Sicily.

Carthage

Although legend attributes the founding of Carthage to its queen Dido, the city was probably established in the late ninth century BC by Phoenician traders. Archaeologists have recovered artifacts there dating to 800 BC. Ideally situated on a peninsula in the Gulf of Tunis, the city had two harbors, linked by canal. By the sixth century BC, Carthage controlled the whole length of the North African coast, from the Atlantic east across the Nile to the farther border of Egypt. It had taken over Libya and the colonies of Phoenicia, the Balearic Islands, Malta,

The theater of
Tauromenium (Taormina)
on Sicily was originally Greek,
but later rebuilt by
the Romans.

Sardinia, and the western part of Sicily. By the fourth and third centuries BC, it had developed into a powerful trading metropolis, the center of a web of settlements and trading posts. The Carthaginians' only serious competition came from Greece.

Wars began about 409 BC over the island of Sicily, 100 miles (160 kilometers) north. In 408 BC, Gelon, the tyrant king of Syracuse, put down a Carthaginian effort to expand under its general Hamilcar. Suc-

ceeding tyrants from Syracuse (Dionysius the Elder and the Younger and Agathocles) continued the battle as Carthage kept trying. With its final defeat at the hands of Pyrrhus, king of Epirus, Carthage was left in control of the western part of the island; the eastern area was under Greek control. The Carthaginians sought support from anyone fighting the Greeks. They successively befriended the Etruscans and the Romans. When the old Roman Appius Claudius made

sion in the struggles known as the Punic Wars. (*Punic* is a Roman corruption of *Phoenician*.)

The immediate cause of war was insignificant. The Mamertines, Italian mercenaries, had seized the city of Messana and turned it into a pirates' den. Their primary victims were Sicilian Greeks. When the energetic tyrant Hiero came to power in Syracuse, he imposed his authority on all Greeks on the island and assumed the title of king. He pressed the Mamertines so hard that in 264 BC they asked for help from both Carthage and Rome. The rivals each promised aid. When Roman soldiers arrived at the Straits of Messana, they saw a Carthaginian fleet

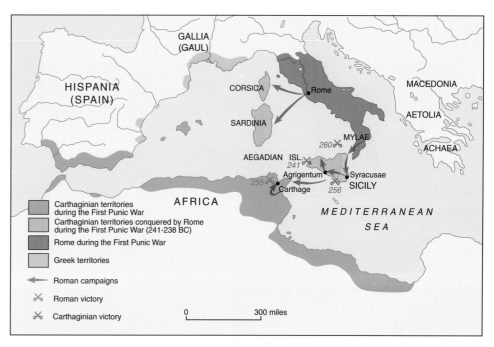

anchored before the city. The Mamertines preferred the Romans and ousted the Carthaginians. Open conflict soon erupted and the First Punic War was to rage for the next twenty-three years.

Sicily was the most important arena of battle. Within a year, Hiero took Rome's side against the Carthaginians. With their large fleet, the Carthaginians could only be defeated by breaking their power on the seas. According to legend, a Carthaginian galley (ship) became stranded on the Italian coast. Using it as a model, the Romans learned how to build warships, training their soldiers on shiplike wooden platforms. In 260 BC, Consul Duilius met the Carthaginian fleet at Mylae near the northern coast of Sicily. The warships of the time had a *rostrum* (Latin for *beak*), a long projecting beam, at the bow, used for ramming and sinking enemy ships. Boarding an enemy ship was not considered important, so when the Carthaginian ships closed in on the Roman vessels, they were

The First Punic War (264–241 BC). Syracuse was originally an ally of Carthage (264–263 BC) but changed sides to Rome (263–241 BC).

his famous speech against peace arrangements with Pyrrhus, then commander of Tarentum's forces, a Carthaginian fleet lay at the Tiber River to provide him moral support.

The First Punic War: 264–241 BC

After Tarentum conceded Roman superiority about 272 BC, the Romans had to protect the interest of their new Greek subjects. This soured their relationship with Carthage. Roman aristocrats pressed for new expan-

Detail of a fresco in a bathhouse in Pompeii, with a scene from a naval battle. The Romans used this type of ship against the Carthaginians.

The remains of old Punic graves that were found not very far from modern Tunis

years, mainly on Sicily, where the Carthaginians were forced back to their marine base. They managed to retake supremacy at sea, twice defeating the Romans. Another Roman fleet was destroyed by a storm off the Sicilian coast.

Hamilcar Barca (c. 270–228 BC)

In 247 BC, a new Carthaginian general arrived in Sicily, Hamilcar Barca of the notable Barcas family. Only his son Hannibal would outdo his reputation as a great strategist. Hamilcar played a game of military hide-and-seek with his opponents, raiding the Italian coast from the mountains near Panormus (modern Palermo, Sicily). He caused Rome such loss of men and matériel that it was forced to pull troops out of the port of Lilybaeum (modern Marsala). This freed his supply route, but it was a costly way of waging war. By 241 BC, both Carthage and Rome were close to exhaustion. In desperation, the Roman citizens themselves paid for outfitting one final fleet. Two hundred ships set sail to close off Hamilcar's bases in Drepana and Lilybaeum. The Carthaginians sent a fleet to relieve their general and met the Roman ships at the Aegean Islands. After a fierce battle, the Carthaginians were ultimately destroyed by the Romans. Forced to end the war, they faced punitive conditions for peace. When the cease-fire was signed, the Roman consul and Hamilcar agreed that Carthage would surrender Sicily, release all prisoners, and pay a total of 2,200 golden talents to Rome over a period of twenty years.

When the Roman delegates arrived in Sicily, they set even more stringent conditions on payment of indemnities. They demanded an additional 1,000 talents, half to be paid immediately and the rest over ten years. Carthage had to agree. The debt caused great financial distress. The city

astonished to see the Romans lower boarding bridges. Fully armed legionnaires crossed to the enemy ships and massacred the Carthaginians in man-to-man combat.

Four years later the Carthaginians were defeated again. Their power appeared to be broken and the Romans decided to take an unprecedented gamble. They sent an expeditionary force to North Africa to attack the capital city itself. This turned out to be a disastrous mistake, since the Carthaginians had had their infantry reorganized by the Spartan mercenary general Xanthippus. He dealt the Romans a devastating defeat. The few soldiers to survive the massacre were picked up from the beach by ships but they were caught in a heavy storm and fewer still survived the passage. The war dragged on for thirteen

The Greek theater near Segesta on Sicily. In 261 BC the inhabitants of the city made a pact with the Romans against the Carthaginians.

Aerial view of the remains of the ancient Punic harbor of Carthage

Monument that the Romans erected on the Forum Romanum after Dullius beat the Carthaginians in the battle of Mylae in 260 BC

could not pay the mercenaries it had used to wage the Sicilian campaign. Supported by Libyan slaves, they rebelled. Carthage called on Hamilcar again but he was unable to subdue the rebels until 238 BC. Rome made use of the three years of confusion by seizing Sardinia and Corsica.

Carthage made Hamilcar Barca commander in chief of the army in 237 BC. With Sardinia, Sicily, and Corsica lost to Rome, he went on to the Carthaginian bases in Spain. He spent the next nine years subjugating the Celtic tribes on the Iberian Peninsula and organizing them into an army. When he died in 228 BC, his son-in-law Hasdrubal succeeded him. The new commander continued the Iberian campaigns with the assistance of his eighteen-year-old brother-in-law, Hannibal. Rome thought it advisable to stop this expansion in Spain before Carthage had completely recovered from its defeat. In 226 BC, the Romans forced Hasdrubal to sign a treaty that his troops would not cross the Iberus (Ebro) River. When Hasdrubal was killed by assassins in 221 BC, the army asked Hannibal to assume command. He would almost destroy the Roman state in the next Punic War.

Mare Nostrum

The First Punic War gave Rome its first territory outside the Italian Peninsula. The name *provincia* (provinces) was used for those territories. Corsica, Sardinia, and the Roman part of Sicily were not considered allies but were treated as subjugated areas. Placed under Roman civil servants, they suffered the same conditions as they had under Carthaginian rulers. Every year two new

praetors (officials) were chosen to rule Sicily and the entity comprising Sardinia and Corsica, bringing the number of praetors to a total of four. (Two praetors already existed in the Italian Peninsula who acted as judges for issues between Romans and between Romans and foreigners.)

After the conquest of Sicily, the Romans proudly used the term *mare nostrum* (our sea) for the waters around the Italian Peninsula and their new islands. As Rome's power grew, so did the sea area they claimed. Eventually they called the whole Mediterranean mare nostrum.

The Second Punic War: 218–201 BC

Within two years of taking command, Hannibal took over all territory between the Tagus and Iberus (Ebro) Rivers. He crossed the Ebro to lay an eight-month-long siege to the Roman dependency of Saguntum (Sagunto), south of it. He had inherited a deep hatred for the Romans from his father. Brought up to avenge the defeat of his city, he intended to do just that, and the resistance of Saguntum gave him the opportunity. The city called on Rome for assistance and the senate promised it. Declaring Hannibal's attack a violation of the Ebro treaty, the Romans insisted that the commander be surrendered to them. When Carthage refused, Rome declared war in 218 BC.

Crossing the Alps

Hannibal welcomed the Roman declaration. He did not wait for his opponents to move. He assembled an army of some 40,000 troops and cavalry. Using battle-trained elephants to carry equipment, he set out from

Trade and Manufacture in the Early Roman Empire

Despite the growth of the city of Rome and the Roman Empire, for centuries all manufacturing activities were undertaken by small independent tradesmen. There were other manufacturing centers on the Italian Peninsula, but some of them suffered from the war with Hannibal. While Tarentum never really recovered, Capua continued to show considerable growth despite its political humiliation. In addition to its famous ceramics and bronzes, this city produced furniture and perfumes. In the second century BC, Campania would completely replace Etruria as Italy's manufacturing center.

Although manufacturing was hampered, trade flourished as a result of war and expansion. It was one-sided trade: Italy imported almost everything and exported little. Rome imported large quantities of grain from Sicily. It was the most important buyer of Spanish silver. Slaves were in great demand for working the growing landholdings of the rich and for service in their increasingly luxurious houses in Rome and other cities. The largest international slave markets were in the east. The island of Delos was the most notable after about 167 BC.

The Roman Senate passed a law which formally forbade senators to own ships. As a result, the merchant trade in the Mediterranean remained largely in the hands of the Greeks and Phoenicians. In the second century BC, an increasing number of Italian merchants appeared in the major harbors, including Rhodes, Delos, Corinth, and Alexandria. They usually originated from Campania and the important harbor of Puteoli.

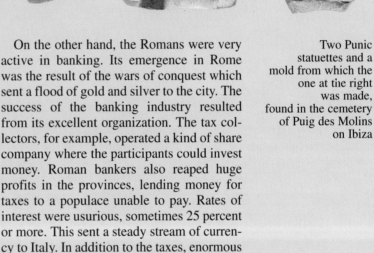

On the other hand, the Romans were very active in banking. Its emergence in Rome was the result of the wars of conquest which sent a flood of gold and silver to the city. The success of the banking industry resulted from its excellent organization. The tax collectors, for example, operated a kind of share company where the participants could invest money. Roman bankers also reaped huge profits in the provinces, lending money for taxes to a populace unable to pay. Rates of interest were usurious, sometimes 25 percent or more. This sent a steady stream of currency to Italy. In addition to the taxes, enormous amounts in reparations were levied on vanquished enemies. A stream of plunder flowed during military campaigns. The spoils of war were divided among all Roman soldiers, but not at the same ratio. The aristocratic officers knew how to enrich themselves better than the common man. Wealthy Romans lent their money out at high interest rates or invested in land. This fostered a rapid growth of large landholdings in Italy. Some of the elite lost interest in political careers and turned to banking and land management. They continued to serve in the army as *equites* (cavalry). Typically, after a period of military service, they would return to their economic activities. These had been forbidden to the senators since 218 BC. This gave rise to a second, politically inactive class. It was called the equites or knights.

Two Punic statuettes and a mold from which the one at the right was made, found in the cemetery of Puig des Molins on Ibiza

Coin from the time of the Roman Republic

The remains of the ancient theater in the city of Saguntum.
In 218, when Hannibal attacked and captured this Spanish city, an ally of Rome, it started the Second Punic War.

New Carthage (modern Cartagena, Spain), headed for Rome. He crossed the Pyrenees Mountains and the Rhône River and marched east along the Mediterranean coast. His plan was to fight the Romans in their own country, expecting that after a decisive victory, Rome's allies would defect to him. The Gallic tribes, recently subjugated by Rome, sent him messengers offering sup-

Bust of Publius Cornelius Scipio, who was nicknamed "Scipio Africanus" because of his campaigns in northern Africa

Bronze helmet
of the type worn by
Scipio's soldiers

port. He had to cross the Alps to reach the Italian Peninsula, with Gallic tribesmen as his guides. It was a harsh expedition, fifteen days long, through snowstorms and avalanches. The army was attacked by huge rocks dropped by mountain-dwelling robbers. Most of the elephants and some 15,000 men died from the cold and starvation.

The Italian Campaigns

By the fall of 218 BC, Hannibal and his army were in the northern part of the Italian Peninsula. He managed to recruit additional troops from the Gallic people called the Insubres. He then conquered their enemies, the Taurini, and formed alliances with the

reluctant Celtic and Ligurian people along the northern Po River. Before the year was over, he defeated a Roman army under Publius Cornelius Scipio (later called Africanus the Elder) at Ticinus (Ticino) and Trebia (Trebbia) in the Po Valley. The road to the south was open.

The next spring, in 217 BC, one Roman consul was with his army on the Adriatic coast. The other, Gaius Flaminius, was in Etruria. Unexpectedly, Hannibal appeared in the region. As soon as he heard that Hannibal was marching south, Flaminius followed with his army. He made forced marches and did not bother to scout the surrounding terrain. In the narrow pass near Lake Trasimenus (Trasimene), Hannibal's forces suddenly surrounded Flaminius's army and wiped it out. Fifteen thousand soldiers died. In Rome, a nervous crowd waited for news. At dusk, the praetor Marcus Pomponius appeared before the senate building and simply said, "A great battle was fought and we were completely defeated." All Rome mourned but there was no panic. The famous patrician Quintus Fabius Maximus Verruco-

Hannibal's soldiers
fought their battles with this
type of Iberian sword.

687

The front of a drachma from New Carthage (Cartagena, Spain), presumably showing the portrait of Hannibal

Coins with the portraits of Ariates IV and Ariates V, the kings of Cappadocia

Marble head of a Carthaginian god

sus was appointed dictator, the special six-month office held only in time of dire emergency.

The Battle of Cannae: August 2, 216 BC

Contrary to expectations, Hannibal did not march on Rome. He crossed the Apennines once more to contact the Greeks and the Samnites on the southern Italian Peninsula, hoping to persuade them to defect. Dictator Fabius followed at a distance, avoiding direct confrontation. Most soldiers didn't agree with this tactic. In Rome, as well, the mood turned more aggressive. Everyone soon called Fabius *cunctator* (dawdler). The dawdler had caused Hannibal serious damage but most Romans did not see it. During the consul elections, the main question was whether or not to risk confrontation. When the subsequent aggressive tactics resulted in catastrophe, many Romans blamed the new people's consul, Gaius Terentius Varro, and painted his new patrician colleague, Lucius Aemilius Paulus, as a man who warned in vain against it. This is almost certainly wrong. Both consuls and most of the senate were in favor of an offensive in 216 BC.

Hannibal had spent the winter at Gerontium, moving his army to Cannae on the Aufidus (Ofanto) River in the spring. When Fabius's six-month term was over, command of the Roman army was given to the new consuls. In the summer they led it toward Hannibal's encampment on the southeastern part of the peninsula. At the end of July, they found him at Cannae, fully prepared. Hannibal had already tested the encircling tactic he used August 2. It was the largest battle in ancient history and the most disastrous defeat Rome had ever suffered. Some 30,000 Romans and allied soldiers died. Aemilius Paulus was killed but Varro escaped with what was left of the army. Hannibal lost some 6,700 men.

Still, Rome did not give in to Hannibal, refusing even to receive his messenger. The city raised new legions and prepared for resistance, but Hannibal was in need of reinforcements that Carthage would not give him. Instead of going to Rome, he tried and failed to take Neapolis (Naples). Capua, the Italian Peninsula's second largest city, opened its gates to him. He wintered there while other cities deserted Rome.

Fighting on Three Fronts

Fabius Cunctator retained his nickname but, after Cannae, the Romans adopted his confrontation-avoiding tactics. They limited themselves to small skirmishes and expeditions to punish deserting allies, but they still ruled the sea. Carthage had difficulty send-

The remains of
some ancient Punic houses
on a hill in Carthage

The head of
Antioch III the Great,
king of Syria

ing reinforcements.

The war was fought on three fronts. On the Italian Peninsula, deserting allies were slowly subjugated. On Sicily, Syracuse had sided with Carthage after Hiero died. In Spain, a Roman expeditionary force under the Scipio brothers harassed Hannibal's brother Hasdrubal (not to be confused with his brother-in-law of the same name). In 211 BC, Hannibal attacked Rome but was turned back. The Romans then retook Capua, starving it into submission with Hannibal unable to help. This cost him the support of many of his other Italian allies. Rome then took Syracuse through treason, despite the ingenious weapons designed by the mathematician-physicist Archimedes. The same year also brought a major defeat for the Spanish army. Both Scipios were killed.

The Battle of Metaurus (Metauro) River

In 210 BC, Publius Cornelius Scipio, son of one of the Scipio brothers, declared his candidacy for the command in Spain. Although he was only twenty-five, he had served in northern Italy against Hannibal and had held

Punic terra-cotta statuette depicting a woman riding a dolphin

the office of *aedile* (official in Roman Republic). His candidacy was accepted. The *comitia centuriata* (assembly) granted him the command and the rank of proconsul. This gave him the same authority as a consul. He quickly restored the morale of the defeated troops in Spain, leading them to one victory after another. In 209 BC, he took New Carthage (present-day Cartagena) where Hannibal's brother Hasdrubal had his headquarters, arsenals, and main base of supplies. Unable to continue, the Carthaginian abandoned Spain. In 207 BC, he decided to try his brother's tactics, attacking the Italian Peninsula through the passes in the Alps. However, the mood had changed in

Gallia Cisalpina. The northerners now took little notice of Hannibal and gave the new invader no help. Hasdrubal was surprised by a Roman legion under Consul Gaius Claudius Nero at the Metaurus (Metauro) River, just south of the Po. His army was annihilated and he was killed. The Romans informed Hannibal of the defeat by throwing his brother's head into a Carthaginian camp.

The Battle of Zama: 202 BC

Scipio returned to Rome in 205 BC, where he was elected consul. He took his army to Africa. Over the next two years, he helped the Numidian leader Masinissa against his tribal rival and defeated Carthage at Campi Magni (today's Suk al-Khamis, Tunisia). Hannibal was recalled to Carthage to help in 203 BC. He set sail from the Greek town of Croton and left a report of his campaign on the local altar to Hera. The historian Polybius was to read it later. In 202 BC, Hannibal visited Scipio in his tent to discuss a number of peace proposals. Scipio would not accept them and Hannibal decided to risk everything in a final battle. The battle was fought on October 18 and was named for the distant town of Zama. Hannibal's new recruits fled, deserting to Rome, and Masinissa's cavalry cut down his veterans. Scipio's victory ended the Second Punic War and earned him the surname Africanus the Elder. He is considered the most important Roman general prior to Caesar. Carthage was forced to surrender the next year.

Carthage Conquered

The conditions of the peace treaty concluded in 201 BC required Carthage to yield Spain to Rome, dismantle its fleet, and pay 10,000 gold talents within fifty years. It was forbidden to wage war outside of Africa and, within Africa, only with Rome's permission.

Hannibal took on a political role, amending the constitution of Carthage and reforming its corrupt government and financial system. Rome regarded his efforts as attempts to break the peace and forced him to flee east. He found safe haven with Rome's enemy, the Syrian king Antioch III the Great, whom he advised in a war against Rome. When Antioch was defeated at Magnesia (Manisa) in 190 BC and pledged to surrender Hannibal to Rome, Hannibal sought sanctuary with Prusias II, the king of Bithynia, a small state in northern Asia Minor. The king, who reigned from 192 to 148 BC, could barely control the pirates on his shores, much less protect Hannibal from the Romans who demanded his surrender. Hannibal resorted to poison. In the end the Romans captured only his body.

Picture of the famous statue of the bronze she-wolf (from the Etruscan period) with Romulus and Remus (added in AD 1510). According to legend, Romulus and Remus were the twin sons of the God Mars by the princess Rhea Silvia. The children were exposed at birth and found and suckled by a she-wolf. Later Romulus became the founder of Rome.

The Roman Revolution

War, Corruption, Uprising, Exploitation

After its victory over Carthage in the Second Punic War in 201 BC, Rome was the preeminent power in the west. The Italian Peninsula was partially destroyed and its population exhausted, but the Roman *oligarchy* (government by a few) had not yet tired of war. The ruling elite wanted to punish the Macedonian king Philip V for his alliance with Hannibal. In 200 BC, it sent a Roman army into Greece, ending Philip's attempt to control the Aegean Sea in 197 BC.

With this victory in the Second Macedonian War (200–197 BC), Rome now dominated the east as well as the west.

Roman armies plunged from one conflict into another. They liberated Greece, allied with it, and marched against Syria's king, Antiochus III. The Romans triumphed at Magnesia in 190 BC and forced the Seleucid Empire into an ignominious peace, taking over its holdings in Asia Minor and Europe. Thousands of people traveled from the

691

Picture of the Clivius Capitolinus, the Roman road that led from the Forum to the Capitol and was used for religious and triumphal processions. The columns of the temple of Saturn are visible in the background.

Italian Peninsula to the Hellenic cities to make their fortunes. Romans became increasingly involved in international trade, giving rise to the nonpolitical class called the *equites* (knights). Most of the wealthy, as well as the senators (who were forbidden to trade), invested their wealth in land in the Italian Peninsula. Land investment was considered morally superior to trade. Prosperity was not universal. War had brought some people great opportunity but ruined many others. While the equites amassed their riches, farmers eked out an existence on the land. Foreign wars called more and more sons away from the land.

The Latifundia

A new form of agriculture developed in rural areas, the *latifundia* (large estates). They were plantationlike operations run by the rich who cultivated grain, wine, and olives with slave labor. Other land, confiscated by the state and occupied by wealthy Romans, was frequently converted to pasture for herds. The shepherds who tended them were often slaves. Small farmers, unable to compete with large landowners, sold out to them and, with nowhere else to go, fled to the city. Hundreds of thousands streamed into Rome.

The city could not handle the invasion.

There was no work. As the proletariat swelled, the rich and powerful profited from the growing empire. *Praetors* (magistrates), expraetors, and exconsuls (one of two annually elected magistrates) were sent to the provinces as governors. One of their tasks was tax collection, which offered great opportunity. Corruption was rampant. Civil servants would lease out the collection of taxes, selling regional concessions for collection at high prices. Equites with a lot of capital formed large consortiums for that purpose, often leasing out part of their licenses, in turn, to *publicans* (tax collectors) who did the actual collecting. Everyone but the taxpayer made significant profit.

Reform Attempts
Marcus Porcius Cato (234–149 BC)
Many people spoke out against the corruption, demanding a return to the senatorial traditions of integrity. The most famous of them was the reputable Marcus Porcius Cato, called Cato the Elder. He was a prosperous gentleman farmer, once given a triumphal Roman celebration for his military service in Spain. He had served as *quaestor* (financial adviser) in 204 BC, as *aedile* (temple functionary) in 199 BC, as praetor in 198 BC, and as consul in 195 BC. As censor in 184 BC, he suspended any senator he considered immoral or unworthy of office. His insight, however, did not extend to the economy. Opposed to Greek influence on Rome, he believed that most of the city's problems could be solved by a return to ancient traditions. Cato was sent to Africa in 157 BC as mediator in a conflict between Carthaginians and Numidians. He came back convinced that Carthage was an even worse threat to Rome than Greece. Until his death he closed every speech with the words, *"Delenda est Carthago"* ("Carthage must be destroyed"). His considerable influence helped bring on the Third Punic War, which did just that.

Tiberius Sempronius Gracchus (c. 163–133 BC)
Other agitation for reform came from some of Cato's worst enemies, an influential liberal faction in the senate led by Sempronius

Statue of a vestal virgin standing in the *Atrium Vestae*. The vestal virgins tended to the sacred fire in the temple of the goddess Vesta. The Romans believed that disaster would come to Rome, if the sacred fire went out.

The Forum Romanum with the *Atrium Vestae* (foreground). The *Atrium Vestae* was a walled garden inside the house of the vestal virgins. The three columns in the background are all that is left of the temple of Castor and Pollux.

693

Roman memorial
statue representing a
husband and wife, dressed in
togas. The statue dates
from c. 75–50 BC.

22

Gracchus, with his two sons, Tiberius and Gaius. Tiberius and Cato did agree on at least two points, Carthage and corruption. In 146 BC, Tiberius was said to have been the first Roman to climb the city wall of Carthage in the battle that destroyed it. As quaestor to the Roman army in Spain in 137 BC, he saved 20,000 defeated troops from slaughter by negotiating with the victorious city of Numantia. Returning to Rome, he saw that Roman society had disintegrated into a small group of corrupt rich people and masses of rootless small farmers. The depopulated rural areas had to be repopulated, which could only be accomplished by offering the peasants land. State land appropriated illegally by large landowners had to

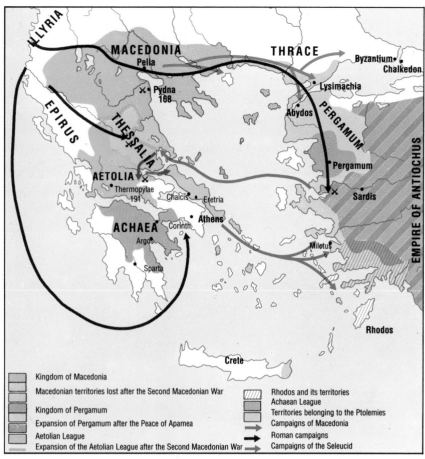

The expansion of the
Roman Empire in the East
(200–146 BC)

be expropriated and redistributed. With this program in mind, Tiberius presented himself as a candidate for the people's tribunal.

He was elected in 133 BC, and put through a law for the just distribution of public land to peasants. The aristocratic senators, led by his own cousin, Scipio Africanus the Younger, not only saw themselves as being robbed of their land, but suspected that Tiberius wanted to form his own army of clients. They convinced another tribune to veto the law as well. However, Tiberius was not deterred. He simply convinced the assembly to remove the troublesome tribune. This action was unheard of, but Tiberius argued that it was as necessary as the driving out of the kings and said the interests of the people took precedence over the immunity of the tribune. This time the assembly accepted the land reform without difficulty.

Tiberius, his brother, and his father-in-law Appius Claudius Pulcher were asked to form a commission to implement it. They were sabotaged on all sides by the senate. Tiberius proposed using the money from the new province of Asia for the land reform. That

Marble statue
depicting a Roman patrician
holding the portraits of two of his
ancestors from the first century BC

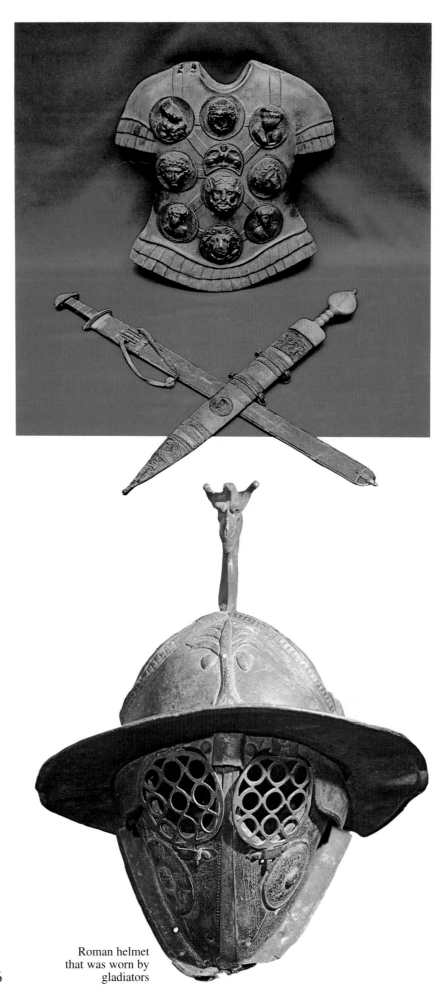

Replicas of a breastplate and swords dating from the first century BC

Roman helmet that was worn by gladiators

irritated the senate, which considered governing the provinces its own prerogative. When his term of office expired, Tiberius stood for an unprecedented reelection. Several radical senators armed their slaves and clients and beat him to death, throwing his body into the Tiber. Three hundred of his followers met similar deaths.

The Roman state was divided the same year, 133 BC. The senate split into the progressive *populares* (advocates of the people) who wanted to follow the path of Tiberius, and the conservative *optimates* (the best) who wanted the senate to retain all power. The senate continued to govern unimpeded. The land reform law was left in place, but little was done with it. The Italian allies were afraid of losing their land. Now that Rome was a world power, they wanted to reap the benefits and sought civil rights as Romans.

Gaius Sempronius Gracchus (c. 153–121 BC)

In 123 BC, the assembly elected Gaius Gracchus tribune of the people. His many proposals had one objective: weakening the power of the optimates. He tried to get the equites behind him, making sure they provided the jury for the court which handled appeals of provincials against Roman civil servants, the prerogative of the senate nobility. It allowed the equites the opportunity to intimidate their superiors in the provinces.

Gaius then established the *lex frumentaria* (grain law), the distribution of grain by the state to the citizens for a fixed price, subsidized by the government. He pursued an active policy to relocate the rootless people of Rome's streets to new colonies, including the ruins of Carthage. Gaius Gracchus was reelected without difficulty in 122 BC. The optimates divided his followers over the issue of civil rights for the Italian allies. Gaius wanted to grant them; most Romans did not. He was not elected for a third term. The senate canceled the colonization of Carthage, claiming that the city was eternally cursed. Without the protection of office, Gracchus was open to attack and hired a private bodyguard. The death of a servant of the consul in a riot provided the optimates a pretext to have the senate declare the state in danger. The consul assembled a vigilante patrol. It defeated Gracchus and his guards in a great fight on the Aventine Hill, the old refuge of the plebeians. Three thousand of his followers were killed. Gracchus was stabbed to death by a faithful slave.

The senate had triumphed, but what Rome needed was a new constitution. The old form of government, adequate for running a city, was not suitable now that Rome had become a world power. It was impossible to govern with new consuls every year, a council of corrupt aristocrats, and a chaotic assembly.

The Third Macedonian War: 171–167 BC

In the beginning of the second century BC,

Rome was satisfied with humiliating the conquered and forcing them to pay huge sums. But the hatred against imperial Rome in Macedonia and later in the Greek world became so strong that new wars were inevitable. Rome battled Macedonia from 215 BC to 168 BC in three different wars. The third war broke out in 171 BC when Perseus, the son and successor of Philip V, led Macedonia against Rome. In 168 BC the Roman general Lucius Aemilius Paulus van-

Temple on the *Forum Boarium* in Rome. It was built c. 100 BC and is a typical example of a platform temple.

Ruins of Numantia
in Spain. The Roman general
Scipio beleaguered this
city for nine months
and completely destroyed
it in 133 BC.

quished Perseus's army and took him prisoner at the Battle of Pydna. The country was divided into four republics under the peace of 167 BC. Following an uprising in 148 BC, Macedonia was made a Roman province.

The European part of Greece followed two years later, after a bitter war in which the wealthy port of Corinth was leveled. Not long thereafter, the Roman Empire expanded into Asia Minor, when the king of Pergamon left his kingdom to Rome in his will in 133 and, after a rebellion, it became the Roman province of Asia.

The Third Punic War (150–146 BC)

Carthage had been battered in 201 BC, but began to flourish again in the second century thanks to its trade, arousing the suspicion and envy of Cato and other conservative Romans. A reason for war was invented, and

cy for twenty-five years. Since he had inherited the name Africanus from his grandfather, the territory became the new province of Africa.

Further Roman Expansion: 133 BC
The Romans had divided Spain into two provinces, but the mismanagement of the

Roman memorial statue representing a married couple (sometimes mistakenly identified as Cato and Porzia), from the first century BC

provincial governors led to almost twenty years of guerilla wars, characterized by treachery, bribery, and cruelty. It's no wonder that governmental service in Spain was unpopular among Roman citizens. One of the centers of resistance to Rome was the small northern city of Numantia, chief stronghold of the Celtiberians (Celts living on the Iberian Peninsula). Scipio Aemilianus, who had been made Roman consul in 134 BC, blockaded the city which surrendered and was destroyed in 133 BC. Scipio was then entitled to add the name Numantinus.

Marius: A New Man, a New Power
Toward the end of the second century BC, Rome again became involved in a war full of scandals. During a civil war, the Numidian king Jugurtha massacred many Italian mer-

the Third Punic War—actually one long siege of Carthage—began in 149 BC. The man in command was the consul Publius Cornelius Scipio Aemilianus, a son of the victor of Pydna and the adopted grandson of Scipio the Elder (of the same full name) who had earlier destroyed Carthage. In 146 BC he destroyed the city again, selling its surviving inhabitants into slavery. He cursed the ruins, pouring salt on them, and forbid reoccupan-

Marble relief from Rome, representing a so-called *suovetaurilia*, an offering of pig (*sus*), sheep (*ovis*), and bull (*taurus*). Dating from the first century BC, it probably belonged in the Temple of Neptune.

Example of a Roman portrait dating from the late republic (late second century BC), identified as Gaius Marius

position of senator with Scipio Aemilianus's support. When Marius came into conflict with his superior, the people elected Marius consul. The *comitia tributa* (assembly of the people) sent him as commander in chief to Numidia, an assignment heretofore given only by the senate. Called away for more important tasks in the north, Marius did not finish the war with Jugurtha. Lucius Cornelius Sulla, the conservative scion of an impoverished patrician family, finished his work, persuading Bocchus I, the king of Mauretania (reigning from 111 to 80 BC) and father-in-law of Jugurtha, to hand over the Numidian king to the Roman army in 106 BC. This ended the Jugurthine War but initiated a conflict with Marius. Jugurtha was executed in Rome.

The German Campaigns: 104–101 BC
In the meantime there was trouble for Rome in the north. The Germanic Cimbrians and Teutons completely destroyed a consular army in Gaul and were thought to be heading for Rome when, to everyone's surprise, they marched toward Spain. That gave Rome a respite. In 104 BC, the people elected Marius consul for the second time, hoping he would save them. He immediately formed a new army. For the first time, all the proletarians who wanted to were permitted to serve in it, since the property restriction was lifted. Soldiers received their weapons from the state, which deducted the cost from their pay. After their period of service, they were promised a parcel of land. Most became professional soldiers, completely dependent on their commander for their maintenance and the land promised to them. Marius traveled to southern Gaul with this new army. He

chants in his country. A Roman army was sent to punish him in 111 BC, but the war dragged on because of the bribery and incompetence of the generals. After several years, the consul Metellus was sent to Numidia. He restored order and discipline and began a powerful offensive. Jugurtha knew the terrain better than the Romans, however, and managed to stay out of their hands. Metellus had a capable adjutant in Gaius Marius, an eques who had risen to the

destroyed the Teutons at Aquae Sextiae in 102 BC and the following year he defeated the Cimbrians at Vercellae on the northern Italian Peninsula. He sent the survivors to the slave market. Marius's new method of recruiting had proven effective, but it would presently become apparent that the soldiers could also be used against the state, since their strongest bond of personal loyalty was to their commander.

The Social War (90–88 BC)

Back in Rome, Marius threw himself into domestic politics, associating himself with the people's party. Its leaders became increasingly radical, and in 100 BC, Marius, as consul, was forced to suppress riots, costing him significant popularity among the people. Although he continued to lead the populares, he was widely mistrusted.

The optimates took over, misusing their power scandalously. In 91 BC they murdered the reform-minded tribune Marcus Livius Drusus who had demanded civil rights for the Italian allies. As a result, most of the allies revolted. The revolutionaries even founded another capital, which they called Italia, governed by a senate and magistrates like those in Rome. Their armies repeatedly defeated the Romans. After two years of fighting, the Romans ended the revolt by granting full civil rights to the inhabitants of every city that surrendered, finally uniting the Italian Peninsula south of the Po in 89 BC.

Lucius Cornelius Sulla, called Felix (138–78 BC)

Since Sulla had provided significant leader-

ship in the Social War, Rome rewarded him with the consulship in 88 BC. The same year, Mithridates VI, the ambitious king of Pontus, came into conflict with Rome. His armies entered the Roman province of Asia, where the population received them as liberators. Sucked dry for almost forty years by tax levies and merciless moneylenders, the aggrieved populace now made short work of its exploiters, killing some 80,000 Italians. Sulla was given command by the senate, over the objections of Marius. The populares, with the support of many equites, pushed through democratic reforms and invested Marius with Sulla's command. Civil war ensued. Sulla took his professional

Reconstruction of a typical Roman house: 1. Shops on the street side; 2. *Vestibulum* (entrance of the house); 3. *Atrium* (central hall with an opening in the roof under which was the *impluvium,* or basin, for rain); 4. *Cubicula* (bedrooms); 5. *Tablinum* (living room); 6. *Triclinium* (dining room used during winter); 7. *Culina* (kitchen); 8. *Balnaeum* (bathroom); 9. *Triclinium* (dining room used during summer); 10. *Gynaeceum* (women's quarters); 11. *Exedra* (sunroom); 12. *Peristylum* (interior garden with columns); 13. *Diaetae* (living rooms used during summer); 14. *Posticum* (back entrance).
During the first century BC the Roman house was sometimes enlarged with a peristylum, next to the atrium. During the reign of Emperor Augustus this peristylum became the most important place in the house.

army to Rome, occupied the city and drove out Marius and his peoples' party in 86 BC. The optimates were restored to power and Sulla was confirmed in his command. He then departed for Pontus in the east.

Scarcely had Sulla disappeared from the Italian Peninsula, when the members of the resistance raised an army of people's party followers in Etruria and occupied Rome. Marius was brought back and elected consul. He was an embittered man, beginning to show signs of madness. There was little regret when he died in 86 BC.

Sulla continued the war against Mithridates. In 85 BC, he forced him into

Marble relief from
the first century BC that was
found in France,
depicting a Gallic warrior
on horseback

peace and the payment of a considerable war retribution. He also made the eastern provinces pay 20,000 talents for their cooperation with the enemy. They had to borrow it from Roman bankers at exorbitant rates of interest. Now Sulla had time to concern himself with his opponents in Rome. In 83 BC he landed at Brundisium and began heavy fighting that lasted a year. In 82 BC, he occupied Rome and had himself appointed dictator. He took the name *Felix* (happy) and, with the optimates, meted out a terrible vengeance after defeating the Samnites at the Battle of the Colline Gate. He instituted a purge of his opponents, condemning them to death or banishment in a reign of terror. He had proscription lists published: anyone whose name appeared on them lost all his possessions and could be killed at any time. Sulla's followers ruled the city.

As self-appointed "dictator to write laws and to organize the state," Sulla reorganized government. He reformed the constitution, attempting to reintroduce the traditional power of the senate and aristocracy. Not an absolute ruler out of personal ambition, he was a member of the senate nobility and wanted to restore its former exclusive power. Tribunes were no longer allowed to introduce bills in the assembly, or to serve in other political positions after their term of office. Equites disappeared from the courts. Individuals were permitted to return to the same office only after intervals of ten years. New laws were introduced in 81 BC that reorganized the criminal justice system. The number of *quaestiones perpetuae* (Rome's first permanent criminal courts) was increased. When he had sufficiently strengthened the power of his class, Sulla withdrew from the political stage. In 79 BC he resigned the dictatorship and retired to an estate in Campania to write his memoirs. (They have never been found.) He died the next year.

Had Sulla saved the republic? He had put power more firmly than ever into the hands of a corrupt collegium of optimates. His measures were forced upon the people. The aristocrats he wanted in power were hated more than ever. It was clear that the republic could not survive in this form. The revolution that had begun with the Gracchi brothers and with Marius was not yet over.

Portrait of Sulla,
who was dictator of Rome
in the first century BC

TIME LINE

	THE GREEK WORLD POLITICAL HISTORY	THE GREEK WORLD CULTURAL HISTORY	EVENTS IN THE REST OF THE WORLD

BC

500

495

490

485

480

475

470

465

460

455

450

445

440

435

430

425

420

415

410

405

400

395

385

380

THE GREEK WORLD POLITICAL HISTORY

499 Ionian rebellion initiates Persian War

490 Battle of Marathon; Athenian army, unaided by its ally Sparta, battles Persian force three times its size

480 Naval Battle of Salamis (Gulf of Aegina); decisive battle of the Persian War; 400 Greek ships, under Athenian Themistocles, defeat 1200 Persian vessels
478/7 Foundation of the Delian League

ca. 460-445 Increasing conflicts between Sparta and Athens
ca. 460-ca. 400 Thucydides, Greek historian, author of *History of the Peloponnesian War*
460 Pericles made leader of popular party and head of state in Athens

445 Thirty-years Peace between Sparta and Athens

431-404 Peloponnesian War between Sparta (with Dorian allies) and Athens (with Ionian allies)
429 Death of Pericles; Cleon succeeds to power in Athens

424 Historian Thucydides made an Athenian general; banished for twenty years for failure in Peloponnesian War
422 Death of Cleon, succeeded by Nicias and Alcibiades in Athens
421 Peace of Nicias
420 Alcibiades elected general in Athens
418 Resumption of Peloponnesian War
415 Athenian fleet departs for Sicily
413 Athenians defeated at Syracuse
404 End of Peloponnesian War; Athens captured, its fleet destroyed by Lysander, death of Alcibiades, end of Athenian democracy; start of oligarchy under the "Thirty Tyrants," end of the Delian League, Spartan hegemony in Greece
403 Civil war ends rule of Thirty Tyrants, democracy restored, popular assembly controlled by orators
399 Agesilaus, king of Sparta, tries to free Greek areas in Asia Minor from Persian control
396-394 Spartan campaigns in the Bosporus and Meander Valley, Asia Minor
395-87 The Corinthian War

387 Peace of Antalcidas (or Kings' Peace) dictated by Persia between Sparta and the coalition of Athens, Thebes, Argos, and Corinth

THE GREEK WORLD CULTURAL HISTORY

485-406 Euripides

455 Euripides's *Peliades*
470-399 Socrates

459-399 Thucydides, first modern historian
ca. 459-380 Lysias the logographer
ca. 457-385 The comedy lyricist Aristophanes expresses his political and social views
441 Euripides wins first prize at the Athenian contest of the celebration of Dionysus with the play *Cyclops*
436-338 Isocrates, orator and logographer
431 Euripides's *Medea*
431-404 Destruction of Athens's harvest by the Spartans, resulting in an increase of the Athenian imports, increase of the city's population; mercenaries, and guerilla tactics determine the war
430-429 Plague epidemic in Athens induces immoral behavior
ca. 425 Completion of the temple of Athena Nikè and the Erechtheum on the Acropolis
ca. 420-350 Isaios the logographer
413 Euripides's *Electra*
412 Lysias returns to Athens from Italian Peninsula

ca. 400-325 Diogenes of Sinope, lifestyle of the cynics

387 Plato founds his Academy in Athens
384-322 Demosthenes, orator and logographer, Aristotle defends the empirical approach
ca. 380 Athens no longer plays an important political role, but continues as a wealthy commercial city with a flowering culture

EVENTS IN THE REST OF THE WORLD

ca. 450 Laws of the Twelve Tablets

395 Gauls plunder Rome and besiege Capitoline Hill

375 Rome has hegemony in the Latin League

Prehistory	Antiquity	Middle Ages	Renaissance	Modern History	Contemporary History

703

THE GREEK WORLD POLITICAL HISTORY	THE GREEK WORLD CULTURAL HISTORY	EVENTS IN THE REST OF THE WORLD

BC

370

365

360

355

350

345

340

335

330

325

325

320

315

310

305

300

290

280

270

260

240

220

200

180

160

THE GREEK WORLD POLITICAL HISTORY

371 Battle of Leuctra, Sparta defeated, hegemony of Thebes

362 Theban army defeated at the Battle of Mantinea; Theban leader Epaminondas killed in battle
359 Philip II made king of Macedonia

338 Battle of Chaeronea, Philip II of Macedonia defeats the Greek allies
336 Alexander succeeds Philip II, after he was murdered
335 Alexander the Great pacifies the north, then destroys rebellious Thebes, Greek city-states surrender
334 Alexander the Great invades Asia Minor, battle of Granicus
333 Battle of Issus, rule over all of Asia Minor
332 Capture of the city of Tyre after a seven-month siege
332-331 Alexander the Great invades Egypt
331 Alexander and his army cross the Euphrates and Tigris Rivers, battle of Gaugamela, conquest of Mesopotamia
330 Alexander invades Persia proper, fierce resistance, Darius III murdered
329-327 Campaigns of Alexander into Bactria and the Indus Valley

325 Trek by Alexander's army from the mouth of the Indus to the west
324 Mass wedding ceremony in Susa
323 Death of Alexander the Great, Alexander IV and Philip III succeed him, actual power in the hands of army general; diadochs
323-ca. 304 Battle of the diadochs brings about formation of new kingdoms

319 Death of Antipater

ca. 306-31 Hellenistic kingdoms
306 Antigones and Demetrius kings of Asia Minor, dynasty of the Antigonids
305 Ptolemy king of Egypt, Palestine, Cyprus, and Cyrenaica, founder of the dynasty of the Ptolemies
305-304 Seleucus II, founder of the dynasty of the Seleucids, king from Sardis to Kabul
305-297 Cassander king of Macedonia

283 Antigonus Gonatas king of Macedonia

260-219 Cleomenes causes social revolution in Sparta

167 Jewish rebellion in Palestine; Judas Maccabaeus

THE GREEK WORLD CULTURAL HISTORY

366-347 Plato's *Theory of Ideas*
ca. 365-275 Pyrrho of Elis founds the School of the Skeptics

ca. 355-280 Herophilus studies the brain and the circulatory system
ca. 350 Xenophon, Demosthenes presents oratories against the military usurper from the north

ca. 341-270 Teachings of Epicurus

ca. 335-263 Zeno of Cition; teachings of the Stoa

331 Foundation of Alexandria in Egypt by Alexander the Great, who emphasizes his descendance from the gods
330 Palace of Persepolis in Persia destroyed by fire

324 Mass wedding to create a mixed Macedonian-Persian elite

ca. 320-305 Foundation of the *Mouseion* in Alexandria

ca. 306-31 Forceful process of Hellenization, Greek generally used as spoken language, cross fertilization of Greek and native cultures; oppression of Jewish culture, rise of the king's cult, adoption of gods from the east, rise of a new wealthy class and impoverization of the population accompanied by inflation, migration toward the east
ca. 300 Euclid's *Elements* (thirteen volumes)
ca. 287-212 Law of Archimedes
ca. 275 Playwright Theocritus writes about life in Alexandria, Aristarchus places the sun at the center of the universe, Erasistratus recognizes the pumping function of the heart
ca. 275-194 Erathosthenes calculates the earth's circumference

ca. 150-100 Hero's steam turbine

EVENTS IN THE REST OF THE WORLD

372-289 Mencius
367 Roman plebeians are admitted to the office of consul

348 Treaty between Rome and Carthage

324-185 North and central India ruled by the Maurya

ca. 300 Majority of Roman Senate consists of plebeians
290 Samnites defeated by Rome
287 *Lex Hortensia* introduced in Rome
ca. 270 Italian Peninsula south of the Po River in Roman hands
264-241 Start of the First Punic War
ca. 250 Rise of the Yayoi culture in Japan; Buddhism in Sri Lanka
221 End of the warring states; King Zheng of Qin in China
218 Hannibal marches over the Alps; start of the Second Punic War
209 Scipio captures Carthago Nova
ca. 200 Teotihuacán grows into a city
ca. 190 Rome eclipses all Hellenistic empires
167 Delos becomes center of international trade

Prehistory	Antiquity	Middle Ages	Renaissance	Modern History	Contemporary History

THE ROMAN WORLD POLITICAL HISTORY	THE ROMAN WORLD CULTURAL HISTORY	EVENTS IN THE REST OF THE WORLD

BC

ca. 1550 Earliest settlement on the site of subsequent Rome

ca. 1500 Indo-European people invade Italian Peninsula

ca. 1000 Another Indo-European people, the Sabines, invade Italian Peninsula

ca. 900-600 Several settlements on the hills surrounding Rome

925-587 Divided kingdom of Israel and Judah in Palestine

753 Traditional founding of Rome by Romulus

ca. 700-600 Latium becomes an undeveloped agricultural area

ca. 625 Valley between Palatine and Capitoline Hills, origin of the settlement of Rome, is built up; controlled by king and Senate

616-509 Last three Etruscan kings rule Rome

ca. 600 Flowering and expansion of Etruria

ca. 700-600 Etruscans adopt the Greek alphabet and several Greek gods

ca. 600 Population increase in Latium, villages become fortified towns, Etruscan kings introduce the *fasces*; two estates in Roman society: patricians and plebeians

ca. 550 The valley between the Capitoline and Palatine Hills is used as a market place: Forum Romanum

ca. 535 Etruscans and Carthaginians drive the Greeks from Corsica

509 End of Etruscan power, start of the Roman Republic, power in the hands of two consuls, the senate and the popular assembly

ca. 500 Strike of the plebeians and installation of the *concilium plebis* and the tribunes of the people

493 Rome included in the Latin League

486 Rome defeats the Latin army

ca. 485 Etruscan attack on Cumae fails

ca. 480 The Latin League defeats the Etruscans at Aricia

474 Last major attack of the Etruscans is repelled

ca. 450 Recording of the current common law, drawing of the provocation

ca. 450-400 Introduction of the office of *quaestores* and *aediles* and the *comitia tributa*

437 Abolishment of the ban on marriage between patricians and plebeians

509 Power in the Roman Republic controlled by the highest estate, patron-client system

ca. 500 Forum Romanum being used as cultural and political center

ca. 500–400 Increase in number of Roman citizens

ca. 450 The laws of the Twelve Canons

ca. 400 Romans capture the wealthy Etruscan city of Veii

ca. 400 Land division is accompanied by alleviation of debt; use of a new elite: the *nobiles*

ca. 750 End of the Dark Age, beginning of the Archaic period in Greece

ca. 722-705 Construction of Khorsabad by Sargon II

ca. 660 Legendary foundation of the state of Japan

612 Beginning of the Neo-Babylonian Empire; destruction of Syrian Nineveh

ca. 600 Foundation of Teotihuacán

594 Legal reforms by Solon in Athens

586 Jewish people in Babylonian exile

ca. 560-483 Gautama Buddha preaches in India

559-530 Golden Age of the Persian Empire under Cyrus the Great

551-479 Confucius

521-486 Darius I ruler of the Persian Empire

512 Darius I crosses the Bosporus

510 Political reforms under Cleisthenes in Athens

480-221 Era of the battling states in China

478 Foundation of the Delian League

464 Rebellion of the helots in Messenia

460-429 Pericles Athenian general

431-404 Peloponnesian War between Athens and Sparta

425 Completion of the temple of Athena Nikè and the Erechtheum on the Acropolis

403 Restoration of democracy in Athens

Prehistory	Antiquity	Middle Ages	Renaissance	Modern History	Contemporary History

705

THE ROMAN WORLD POLITICAL HISTORY	THE ROMAN WORLD CULTURAL HISTORY	EVENTS IN THE REST OF THE WORLD

BC

400 — **ca. 400-200** Carthage evolves into a powerful state

399 Death of Socrates

395 — **ca. 395** Gauls plunder Rome and besiege the Capitol

390 —

385 —

380 —

375 — **375** Rome has hegemony in the Latin League

370 —

367 One of the two consuls mandated to be *plebeian*
365 — **366** Introduction of new office of *praetor*

360 —
358 Rome forces all Latins into a closer alliance
356 Appointment of first plebeian dictator
355 —

351 Election of first plebeian as censor
350 —
348 Treaty between Rome and Carthage

ca. 350-250 Size of the army grows, improved weaponry, organization, and tactics

345 —

343-341 Rome fights the Samnites
340 — **340-338** Latin League rises up against Roman domination
338 Dissolution of the Latin League

335 —
336-323 Conquests of Alexander the Great reach as far as India
330 —
326-304 Last war between Rome and the Samnites
331 Foundation of Alexandria in Egypt
325 —
321 Roman army invades the land of the Samnites but is defeated
320 —

315 —

310 — **309** Another Roman army is defeated by the Samnites

305 — **305** Samnites invade Campania but are defeated
304 Peace between Rome and the Samnites; Campania definitively within Rome's sphere of influence
300 — **ca. 300** Plebeian majority in the senate
ca. 300-275 Roman population divided in five categories of wealth
295 — **295** Samnites defeated definitively by Rome

ca. 300-200 Roman weaponry gradually becomes more uniform

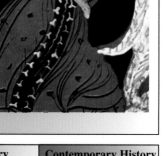

290 —

287 *Lex Hortensia*, decisions by the *concilium plebis* equal to those of the *comitia centuriata* and *tributa*
285 —

280 — **280/279** Pyrrhus victorious in Heraclea and Asculum over the Romans

275 — **275** Rome defeats Pyrrhus at Malventum

Prehistory	Antiquity	Middle Ages	Renaissance	Modern History	Contemporary History

THE ROMAN WORLD POLITICAL HISTORY	THE ROMAN WORLD CULTURAL HISTORY	EVENTS IN THE REST OF THE WORLD

BC

270

ca. 270 Italian Peninsula south of the Po in Roman hands, worsening relations with Carthage

265

264 Mamertines call in the assistance of Rome and Carthage
264-241 First Punic War, Sicily is the major theater of war

260

260 Victory by consul Duilius at Mylae

255

256 Carthaginians again defeated, Rome sends army to attack Carthage, resulting in fiasco

250

247 Carthaginian general Hamilcar lands in Sicily

ca. 250 Rise of the Yayoi culture in Japan; Buddhism in Sri Lanka

245

240

241 Carthaginians defeated near the Aegadian Islands; uprising in Sicily; Rome annexes Corsica and Sardinia; first Roman province

ca. 240 Livius Andronicus produces Latin versions of Greek plays

235

230

225

226 Treaty with the Carthaginians stipulating that the Ebro River will not be crossed

220

221 Hasdrubal is murdered, is succeeded by Hannibal

221 End of the warring states; King Zheng of Qin in China

218-201 Second Punic War; Rome declares war with Carthage, Hannibal marches over the Alps and defeats a Roman army in the Po Valley
217 Consul Flaminius and his army defeated by Hannibal

215

216 Biggest Roman defeat at Cannae, Hannibal captures Capua
215-205 First Macedonian War

ca. 218-200 Destruction and depopulation of southern Italian Peninsula, economic chaos, strong decline in agricultural production
218 Senators forbidden to own seagoing vessels, commercial shipping largely controlled by Greeks and Phoenicians

210

211 Syracuse and Capua captured by the Romans, Roman army defeated in Spain, Publius Cornelius Scipio becomes consul
209 Scipio Africanus captures Carthago Nova
207 Romans defeat the army of Hasdrubal at Metaurus

ca. 210 Capua flourishes, manufacturing ceramics, bronze, perfume, and furniture; trade increases, especially in grain and slaves; monetary market develops

205

204 Scipio and his army invade Africa
203 Hannibal is called back to Carthage
202 Scipio Africanus wins major victory at Zama
201 Carthage gives up the battle, end of the Second Punic War

200

200-197 Second Macedonian War; Macedonian king Philip V defeated by the Romans

ca. 200 Influenced by Hellenistic sculpture, realistic portraiture evolves

Prehistory	Antiquity	Middle Ages	Renaissance	Modern History	Contemporary History

THE ROMAN WORLD POLITICAL HISTORY	THE ROMAN WORLD CULTURAL HISTORY	EVENTS IN THE REST OF THE WORLD

BC

190

ca. 190 Rome eclipses all Hellenistic empires

ca. 190 Flowering of international trade and of the *equites* class

185

180

ca. 179 Construction of the *Basilica Aemilia* on the Forum Romanum

175

175 Huge migration of peasants into Rome, growth of the proletariat

171-167 Third Macedonian War

ca. 170-86 Lucius Accius, poet and dramatist, *Medea* and *Philocteta*

170

168 Roman Aemilius Paullus defeats Macedonian army
167 Macedonia divided in four republics

167 Delos is a center of the international slave trade

167 Jewish uprising in Palestine; Judas Maccabaeus

165

160

155

150

150-146 Third Punic War
148 Macedonia loses a rebellion; annexed as a Roman province
146 European part of Greece made a Roman province, Carthage seized
143-133 Town of Numantia in northern Spain resists Roman armies

146 Corinth demolished

145

140

135

133 King of Pergamon bequeaths his empire to Rome, made Roman province of Asia; Tiberius Gracchus becomes tribune of the people, Senate divided in *optimates* and *populares*

130

125

123 Gaius Gracchus becomes tribune of the people, wants to weaken the power of the optimates
122 Gaius Gracchus reelected
121 Death of Gaius Gracchus and his followers

120

115

111 War with Numidia

110

107 Army reforms by Marius

105

106-43 Cicero

102 Marius destroys the Teutons
100 Marius loses popularity quelling riots

100

ca. 100 Cato, *Lydia*, *Diana*, and *Origines*
ca. 100-50 Rise of black-and-white floor mosaics

100 Construction of the Pyramid of the Sun in Teotihuacán

95

91 Optimates murder reformist tribune Drusus

90

89 Italian Peninsula south of River Po finally united
88 Mithridates welcomed as a liberator in Asia, Sulla advances to Rome
88-82 Civil war in the Roman Empire and also wars against Mithridates in Asia Minor
86 Death of Marius

85

83 Sulla lands in Brundisium
82 Sulla occupies Rome as a dictator, Senate obtains all powers

80

ca. 80 First of Cicero's oratories

79 Sulla withdraws from politics
78 Sulla dies

75

ca. 75 Construction of the theater in Orange

Prehistory	Antiquity	Middle Ages	Renaissance	Modern History	Contemporary History

Glossary

Achaean League alliance of city-states in province of ancient Greece called Achae; had limited autonomy; federal government determined its foreign policies; dissolved in 146 BC and made a dependency of Rome.

aedilis government official in the Roman Republic; oversaw public order, the market, water and grain supplies, and games. Initially, aediles were officers at the temple of Diana in the Latin League.

Aeschylus (525-456 BC) Greek writer of tragedies.

Aetolian League alliance of autonomous Greek city-states around Aetolia.

Agesilaus king of Sparta (c. 400 BC); described by the historian Xenophon.

Alba Longa city in southern Latium, considered the mother city of Rome; according to legend, freed by Romulus and Remus from a usurper; destroyed around 650 BC by King Tullus Hostilius.

Alcibiades (c. 450-404 BC) wealthy ambitious Athenian; general (420 BC); ended the Peace of Nicias, undertaking the Sicilian expedition. Charged with sacrilege, he defected to Sparta; killed by the Persians.

Alexander the Great (356-323 BC) king of Macedonia (336-323 BC); son of Philip II; conquered the Persian Empire (334-330 BC); conquered Syria and Egypt (333 BC); invaded the Indus Valley (327 BC).

Alexandria city founded in Egypt by Alexander the Great in 333 BC; the name was also given by Alexander to other cities he founded.

Antigonus I (382-301 BC) called Monophthalmus (one-eyed) or Cyclops; king of Macedonia (306-301 BC); a general of Alexander the Great and one of the diadochs; obtained control of much of Asia Minor with the division of Alexander's empire in 323 BC. With his son Demetrius I (Poliorcetes), he invaded Egypt; defeated by an alliance of other diodachs.

Antigonus Gonatas (320-239 BC) son of Demetrius Poliorcetes, king of Macedonia. After a long battle he eventually became king of Macedonia (277-239) and ruler of Greece. The dynasty of the Antigonids ruled Macedonia until the arrival of the Romans in 148 BC.

Antioch III the Great (242-187 BC) king of Syria (223-187 BC).

Antipater (c. 398-319 BC) Macedonian general left in charge of Macedonia in 334 BC when Alexander the Great went to conquer the Persian Empire; put down rebellion in Athens after Alexander's death. His descendants ceded power to the Antigonids.

Archimedes (287-212 BC) mathematician and physicist whose theories on natural forces in practice included the principle of displaced water: that a body submerged in a liquid at rest is acted upon by a force equal to the weight of the fluid displaced.

archon (ruler) one of the nine chief magistrates of ancient Athens.

Aristophanes (c. 445-385 BC) Athenian comic dramatist who criticized current political, literary, and social views in fiercely satirical plays about democracy, the war with Sparta, and the Sophists.

Aristotle (384-322 BC) Athenian philosopher, disciple of Plato.

Athens Greek city-state in Attica; progressive, democratic cultural center with an economic basis in trade and an expansionist navy; controlled the Delian League during the Classical period.

Attica Greek state and peninsula on which the polis of Athens lay.

Barsine (?-323 BC) also called Stateira; daughter of the Persian king Darius III; wife of Alexander the Great.

Brasidas important Spartan general, killed with his Athenian enemy Cleon in 422 BC, clearing the way for the Peace of Nicias.

Brutus, Iunius Roman statesman; relative of the last king Tarquinius Superbus; led the revolution against his tyrannical rule and instituted the republic.

Cannae town in southeastern Italy; site of the worst defeat in Roman history; Hannibal surrounded a Roman army and decimated it (216 BC).

Capua major Greek colony in southern Italy; first Greek colony to side with Hannibal in the Second Punic War.

Carthage Phoenician colony on the coast of North Africa (present-day Tunisia); important trading power; rival of Rome in the Punic Wars.

Cato, Marcus Porcius (the Elder) (234-149 BC) Roman statesman and author; served as quaestor (204 BC), aedile (199 BC), praetor (198 BC), consul (195 BC), and most notably as censor (184 BC); combated Hellenism and senatorial corruption.

censor office in the Roman Republic, to which two ex-consuls were elected for five-year terms; they estimated the number of citizens for purposes of categorization, taxation, and military service, and judged moral behavior.

centuria (century) Roman legion of 100 foot soldiers, originally composed of free Romans able to afford armor.

Cimbrians a people who invaded southern France and Spain c. 111 BC; defeated by Marius in 102 and 101 BC.

Classical period period in Greek history (c. 500-334 BC); marked by Persian Wars (492-479 BC) and the Peloponnesian War (431-404 BC).

Cleomenes (235-219 BC) king of Sparta; his forgiving of all debts and redistribution of land caused social unrest in Greece; defeated by Macedonia and the Achaean League.

Cleon (?-422 BC) extremist democratic Athenian politician; rose to power after Pericles's death in 429 BC.

clientes (clients) free, poor and noninfluential Roman citizens, supported financially and legally by rich patrician or plebeian patrons in exchange for votes and services.

comitia centuriata (assembly of centuries) Roman assembly comprising thirty wealthy *centuriae iuniores* (junior centuries) and thirty *centuriae seniores* (senior centuries).

comitia tributa (assembly of tributes or districts) Roman assembly drawn from thirty-five districts; each *tribus* (district) elected tribunes and aediles; introduced in the third and fourth centuries BC.

concilium plebis (council of plebs) Roman popular assembly of plebeians at the beginning of the republic. It elected tribunes able to veto patricians and the senate.

consul highest Roman official. Two consuls were appointed annually to govern the senate and the popular assembly.

Croesus king of Lydia (560-546 BC); noted for his wealth; incorporated all Greece except Samos into the Lydian Empire; overthrown by Cyrus the Great of Persia, in 546 BC.

curia group who ratified the king's election; an assembly with purely ceremonial function and thirty members called *curiae* in the republic of Rome.

Cynics school of philosophy in fourth-century BC Greece founded by Diogenes of Sinope, nicknamed *Kyon* (cur or dog) for his ascetic lifestyle; considered civilization and the material world contemptible; advocated return to a simple, natural life to attain happiness through self-sufficiency and independence.

Darius III (Codomannus) (c. 380-330 BC) last king of Persia (336-330 BC); great grandson of Darius II; handed rule by the eunuch Bagoas, whom he later killed; led the Persians against Alexander the Great; defeated at the battles of Issus (333 BC) and Gaugamela (331 BC); killed by one of his own satraps while fleeing Gaugamela.

De Agri Cultura treatise on farming written by Hippocrates; the oldest surviving prose work in Latin.

Delian League (478-404 BC) voluntary

709

alliance of Athens and Ionian city-states in Asia Minor, Aegean Islands, and colonies in Thrace to rid them of Persians remaining after the Persian War; dominated by Athens; dissolved after the Peloponnesian War.

Demetrius I (Poliorcetes) (?-283 BC) king of Macedonia (294 BC); son of Antigonus Monophtalmus. Defeated with his father at the Battle of Ipsus (Phrygia) by an alliance of diadochs in 301 BC; retained Macedonia and dependent Greek cities for the Antigonid dynasty; imprisoned by Seleucus in 286 BC.

Demosthenes (384-322 BC) Athenian orator, logographer, and politician; led Athenian opposition to Macedonia; renowned for his Philippics, political oratories warning of the rising power of Philip II; urged Athenian alliance with Thebes against Macedonia.

diadochoi (successors) generals who succeeded Alexander the Great upon his death in 323 BC, dividing his empire; their vying dynasties included the Ptolemies, the Antigonids, and the Seleucids.

Diana Roman goddess of the moon and the hunt; identified with the Greek goddess Artemis; worshiped in the Latin League; given a sanctuary on the Aventine Hill in Rome in the late sixth century BC.

dictator Roman magistrate appointed by the senate; given unlimited authority in matters of state and war for six months.

Ebro River river stipulated by treaty after the First Punic War as the border between the spheres of influence of Rome and Carthage.

Epamenondas (?-362 BC) Theban general; broke Spartan hegemony in 371 BC, making Thebes the predominant Greek power for ten years; noted for army reform and introduction of the diagonal phalanx.

Epictetus Greek Stoic philosopher.

Epicurus (c. 341-270 BC) Greek philosopher; taught that goal of life is pleasure regulated by moderation, morality, serenity, cultural development, and freedom from fear of death (since he postulated no afterlife).

equites (horsemen or knights) second rank of Roman society, below senator; of cavalrymen, merchants, and bankers; influential due to financial position and control of taxes.

Eratosthenes (c. 276-c.196 BC) Greek astronomer, mathematician, geographer, and poet in Alexandria, Egypt; noted for his measurement of the circumference of the earth to within 15-percent accuracy.

Etruscans people thought to originate in Asia Minor who settled in central Italy about 800 BC; politically dominant in the sixth century BC.

Euripides (c.485-406 BC) Athenian tragic dramatist; notable for realism and satire of traditional values; works include *Medea*, *Andromache*, and the *Bacchae*.

Fabius, Quintus Maximus (Cunctator) (third century BC) Roman general, dictator in 217 BC; his tactic of avoiding direct confrontation led to Hannibal's defeat in the Second Punic War.

Faiyum oasis lake in Egypt drained to provide fertile land; papyri found here contain text detailing the drainage and exploitation of the area by slaves and leaseholders.

fasces ax bound in a bundle of sticks; symbol of imperial authority in Rome; probably of Etruscan origin.

Gaugamela city in northern Mesopotamia where Alexander the Great defeated the Persians under Darius III in 331 BC.

Gauls Celtic people who moved westward from central Europe at the end of the sixth century BC; threatened the southern Mediterranean around 400 BC; conquered parts of Etruria, destroyed Rome; were paid ransom to settle in northern Italy.

gens (people) Roman clan led by chieftains, *patres* (fathers) with absolute authority over wives, children, and slaves; later, patres were members of the senate and called patricians.

Gordian knot Greek legend; complex knot tied by King Gordius of Phrygia. According to oracle, he who untied it would rule Asia. Alexander the Great cut it with his sword. "To cut the Gordian knot" means quickly solving a difficult problem.

Gracchus, Gaius Sempronius (?-122 BC) Roman statesman; brother of Tiberius; tribune (123 BC); introduced social reforms; decreased grain prices. When he tried to grant civil rights to the *socii*, riots broke out in which he was killed.

Gracchus, Tiberius Sempronius (?-133 BC) Roman statesman; tribune (133 BC); pushed a land reform plan through the popular assembly. Landowners resisted, street fighting erupted. Gracchus was killed.

Graces the three Roman goddesses of beauty, joy, and charm; daughters of Zeus by the nymph Eurynome. Thalia was associated with good cheer; Aglaia with splendor; and Euphrosyne with mirth.

Granicus River site of the battle in northwestern Asia Minor where Alexander the Great defeated a large Persian army in 334 BC, gaining control of Asia Minor.

Hamilcar Barca (c. 270-228 BC) Carthaginian general; father of Hannibal; commanded Carthaginian forces in Sicily in the First Punic War; defeated by Rome in 241 BC; conquered much of the Iberian Peninsula (237-228 BC).

Hannibal (?-183 BC) Carthaginian general; son of Hamilcar; during the Second Punic War, advanced from Spain to Italy, regularly defeating Roman armies; persuaded the *socii* to defect. In 203 BC, he was forced to defend Carthage against the Romans. After the

peace in 201 BC, he fled from the Romans and committed suicide.

Hellenism Greek civilization especially as modified in the Hellenistic period by oriental influences; a body of humanistic and classical ideals associated with ancient Greece and including reason, the pursuit of knowledge and the arts, moderation, civic responsibility, and bodily development.

Herophilus (c. 335-280 BC), Alexandrian physician, father of human anatomy; first to form conclusions from dissection; recognized that arteries pumped blood, that the brain is the center of the nervous system; identified motor and sensory nerves; described the eye, liver, and genitalia. His works have been lost.

hetairoi personal retinue of the Macedonian king, on equal footing with him and treated as friends; rebelled against Alexander the Great in 324 BC.

Hippocrates of Kos (c. 460-c. 377 BC) Greek physician called the father of medicine; disassociated ancient medicine from superstition, basing it on diagnosis through clinical observation and logic. The Hippocratic Oath is attributed to him, as are some seventy medical works; he probably wrote six.

hoplites Greek foot soldiers, named for the round shields they carried.

Indus River Valley (India) conquered by Alexander the Great (327 BC); the eastern border of his Macedonian empire.

Isocrates (436-338 BC) Athenian orator, logographer, and teacher of eloquence.

Issus coastal city on the border between Syria and Asia Minor where Alexander defeated a large Persian army in 333 BC.

Judas Maccabeus (?-161 BC) from the Hasmonaeans family of Jewish patriots. The Latin surname, probably derived from Aramaic maqqabâ (the Hammerer), gave rise to the English *Maccabee*, applied to Judas's relatives. Notable for his defeat of much larger Syrian armies between 166 and 165 BC. His restoration of Jewish rites to the Temple of Jerusalem (December 165 BC), is commemorated by the Jewish festival Hanukkah.

Jugurtha (?-105 BC) African Numidian king in conflict with the Romans. When Italic merchants were killed during a civil war, Rome retaliated in the Jurgurthian War (112-105 BC). Jugurtha was defeated by Sulla.

Kings' Peace treaty concluded in 387 BC between Sparta and other city-states including Thebes and Athens; written under Persian supervision, it ended Spartan imperialism and began Persian rule of the Ionian cities.

Kings Period era when Rome was ruled by kings: Romulus, Numa Pompilius, Tullus Hostilius, Ancus Martius, and the Etruscans (616-509 BC): Priscus Tarquinius, Servius Tullius, and Tarquinius Superbus.

Latin League ethnic religious federation of Latin cities on the Italian Peninsula; fought the Etruscans in the sixth century BC; abolished in 338 BC, following rebellion against Roman domination.

Latini inhabitants of Latium; lived in small villages on the hills of the Italian Peninsula until the seventh century BC, when the Etruscans took over; thereafter, they lived in *oppida* (fortified towns); formed religious and political alliances, including the Latin League.

Laws of the Twelve Tables Roman common law codified and engraved on twelve bronze plates by the *decemviri* (ten men), a commission of ten patricians, in 451 BC.

logographers orators in Athens who wrote oratories (speeches) for others. During the classical era, orators strongly influenced politics. They were often *metoikoi* (foreigners) not allowed to hold political office.

Lupercalia (wolves' feasts) Roman festival named for the wolves' skins worn by the participating priests.

Lysias (459-380 BC) orator and *metoikos* (foreigner) logographer in Athens; expended his fortune on the revolutionary cause; renowned for his oratory against Eratosthenes, one of the Thirty Tyrants running Athens.

Macedonia ancient kingdom north of Greece. King Philip II expanded Macedonian rule to Greece. His son, Alexander the Great, conquered the Middle East and Egypt. Alexander's successors (the diodachs) fought for power in Macedonia until Antigonus Gonatas founded the dynasty of the Antigonids. Macedonia was divided in four sub- states in 167 BC; all were made a Roman province in 148 BC.

Macedonian Wars between Rome and Macedonia from c. 215 BC for power in Macedonia and Greece.

Mamertines Italian mercenaries and pirates on Sicily; their request for assistance from Carthage and Rome in a conflict with Hero of Syracuse was the immediate cause of the First Punic War.

Marius, Gaius (156-86 BC) Roman statesman; fought the African king Jugurtha (107 BC), the Cimbrians and Teutons (102-101 BC); led the opposition against the senate party and Sulla; his popular party exercised a bloody reign in Rome (87-83 BC); first to equip a professional army of plebeians.

Menander (?-293 BC) Greek playwright of comedy, representative of the new comedy. His plays were known only from imitations by Latin comedic dramatists until the nineteenth century AD, when Greek papyri with fragments of them were found.

metoikoi (foreigners) inhabitants of Athens of foreign origin or descent who had no civil or voting rights and could not occupy government offices but were liable for taxes and army service.

Miletus major city in Ionia.

Mithridates king of Pontus in northern Asia Minor (120-63 BC); led an uprising against Rome in 88 BC in Asia Minor and Greece; defeated by Sulla in 84 BC.

Mouseion (museum) founded in Alexandria by Ptolemy I as a temple to the Muses; center for the arts and sciences.

municipia (towns or municipalities) originally non-Roman Italic cities granted Roman civil rights after being conquered; had local autonomy but no major political influence.

Muses in Greek mythology, nine goddesses who inspired philosophers, poets, musicians, and artists; the daughters of the paramount god Zeus and Mnemosyne, the goddess of memory, each presided over an art or a science. Poetry was so important it had several

muses Polyhymnia for sacred poetry, Calliope for epic poetry, Erato for love poetry, and Euterpe for lyric poetry. Terpsichore was in charge of choral singing and dance, Thalia of comedy, and Melpomene of tragedy. Clio presided over history and Urania over astronomy.

new comedy genre of comedy from the Hellenistic era, characterized by stereotypes; did not satirize or offer political or social criticism; major representative was Menander.

Nicias (?-413 BC) moderate democratic Athenian politician and strategist; negotiated the Peace of Nicias (421-418 BC); reluctantly took part in the Sicilian expedition which ended it; killed by the people of Syracuse.

nobiles (nobles) class in the Roman Republic consisting of patricians and rich plebeians that arose after the equalization of patrician and plebeian power in 287 BC. Consuls and other magistrates were elected from it; it controlled the senate.

oligarchy rule by a few.

oppida small fortified cities ruled by Latini aristocracy; grew from Latin hill towns during political and cultural domination by the Etruscans.

Parthians Persian horsemen who gained their independence from the Seleucids c. 250 BC and settled in northern Persia; conquered extensive territory east of the Seleucid Empire; later fought the Romans.

patricians small group of families in Rome who fulfilled all administrative and religious offices. They based their position of power on their clients. They slowly had to give in to the plebeians. In 207 BC the battle of the various estates ended.

Paulus, Lucius Aemilius (c. 229-c.160 BC) Roman general who defeated Macedonia in 168 BC.

Peloponnesian League military alliance of Peloponnesian city-states between the sixth and fourth centuries BC, dominated by Sparta. In the Peloponnesian War, some members revolted because Sparta threatened their independence.

Peloponnesian War (431-404 BC) conflict of hegemony between Athens, generally allied with Ionians, and Sparta, allied with Dorians. The direct cause was a conflict about Corcyra. The army of Sparta annually destroyed Attica while the Athenian fleet plundered the Peloponnesian coasts. Sparta finally triumphed over Athens with the help of the Persians.

Pericles (?-429 BC) Athenian leader of popular party and head of state (460-429 BC); led Athens to its greatest political, cultural, and architectural achievements.

perioikoi (conquered) the indigenous people of the territory conquered by Sparta.

Perseus (c. 212-c. 166 BC) king of Macedonia; son and successor of Philip V; defeated by Rome in the Third (and final) Macedonian War (171-167 BC).

Persians Indo-Iranian peoples living on the Iranian plateau and mountains. Beginning in the sixth century BC, they created a world empire, subsequently conquered by Alexander the Great in 330 BC.

phalanx battle array used by Greek and Macedonian infantry, consisting of a number of rows of heavily armed soldiers. Thebans introduced the diagonal phalanx, with more rows on one side.

Philip II (382-336 BC) king of Macedonia (359-336 BC); reorganized the army, conquered surrounding regions, and became involved in Greek politics. In 338 BC, he defeated the allied Athens and Thebes.

Philippics Demosthenes's orations against Philip of Macedonia in the fourth century BC.

Pindar (520-440 BC) Greek lyricist from Thebes.

planetes (wanderer) planets; name given by the ancient Greeks to the celestial bodies they saw "wandering" among the fixed stars.

Plato (c. 429-347 BC) Athenian philosopher and disciple of Socrates; wrote philosophical dialogues in which he had Socrates express his own theories.

plebeian member of the ancient Roman lower class; originally, the masses of Rome had no influence but were put on the same level as the patricians in 287 BC. Rich plebeians shared power with patricians beginning in the fourth century BC.

polis (city) independent Greek city-state (plural: *poleis*).

Pomerium sacred precinct of Rome; burial of the dead took place outside it.

praetor Roman official charged with jurisprudence for one year; competent to lead

711

the army; originally appointed as provincial governor.

***proscription* list** system of terror introduced by Sulla (82-78 BC); opponents of his senate party were listed for public persecution. They were exiled or murdered and their possessions were confiscated.

provincia (provinces) territory conquered by Rome outside of Italy; governed and often exploited by (pro)consuls or (pro)praetors. The first provinces were Corsica, Sardinia, and portions of Sicily won from Carthage.

Prusias II king of Bithynia (192-148 BC).

Ptolemy (c. AD 100-c.170) astronomer and mathematician of Alexandria; dominated scientific thought until sixteenth century AD; used geometry to model an earth-centered universe described in the *Almagest*, originally written in Greek. His works include *Optics*, *Harmonica*, *Geography*, and *Tetrabiblos* (on astrology).

Ptolemy I Soter (preserver) (c. 367-285 BC) king of Egypt (323-285 BC), founder of the Ptolemic dynasty; a general of Alexander and one of the diadochs who succeeded him; proclaimed himself king of independent Egypt in 305 BC, expanding it to Palestine and Cyrenaica. His dynasty ruled Egypt until the arrival of the Romans (31 BC).

***publicani* (publicans)** Roman tax collectors.

Punic War, First (264-241 BC) war between Rome and Carthage for supremacy in the western Mediterranean. Rome adopted seafaring armies to defeat the Carthaginian power at sea. By introducing grappling, they defeated the Carthaginians. Carthage then ceded Sicily.

Punic War, Second (218-201 BC); between Rome and Carthage (under Hannibal) for supremacy in the western Mediterranean.

Punic War, Third (150-146 BC) between Rome and Carthage for supremacy in the Mediterranean; the Romans destroyed Carthage in 146 BC.

Pyrrhus (318-272 BC) king of Epirus (319-272 BC); supported Tarentum against the Romans; defeated the Romans albeit with great losses on his side (280-279 BC), leading to the phrase *Pyrrhic victory*.

quaestor Roman official who originally assisted consuls in criminal justice; eventually, financial manager; the office was often the starting point of a political career.

***res publica* (public thing)** republic; Roman state (c. 509-31 BC) governed by two annually elected consuls; citizens exercised influence through popular assemblies and the Senate.

Rome capital of the Roman Empire, located on the Tiber River in Latium; according to legend, founded in 753 BC by Romulus and Remus.

Romulus and Remus legendary founders of Rome.

Roxana (?-c. 311 BC) daughter of Oxyartes of Sogdiana; a Persian wife of Alexander the Great.

Saguntum Spanish city south of the Ebro River; its request for Roman assistance was the direct cause of the Second Punic War.

Samnites mountain people of the southern Apennines; fought Rome and the Latin League (343-341 BC); later supported Rome against the league. After another two wars (326-304 BC, 298-290 BC), they were made allies of Rome.

Scipio Africanus the Elder (Publius **Cornelius Scipio Africanus Maior**) (c. 234-183 BC) Roman general; hero of the Second Punic War against the Carthaginians; made commander of Roman forces in Spain (210 BC); consul (205 BC); defeated Hannibal and the Carthaginians at the Battle of Zama (North Africa) in 202 BC.

Scipio Africanus the Younger (Publius Cornelius Scipio Aemilianus Africanus Numantinus) (c. 185-129 BC) Roman general; adopted grandson of Scipio the Elder; military tribune to Spain (151 BC); commander in the Third Punic War; consul (147 BC) captured and destroyed Carthage (146 BC).

Seleucid Empire eastern portions of Alexander the Great's empire governed by descendants of Seleucus.

Seleucus I (355-280 BC) king of Babylon (312-280 BC); general of Alexander the Great; as one of the diadochs, gained power in Mesopotamia and areas east; expanded west to Syria and Asia Minor; founder of the Seleucid dynasty.

senate college of magistrates, highest authority in the republic of Rome.

Sicilian expedition (415-413 BC) unsuccessful Athenian military campaign to gain hegemony in the Mediterranean.

Skeptics Greek school of philosophy founded around 300 BC; from *skeptikos* (inquiring); denied the possibility of real knowledge; considered inquiry to be always a process of doubting and judgments to have only relative value.

***socii* (allies)** Italian cities subjugated by the Romans and granted limited civil rights and local autonomy. In 91 BC they revolted, gaining full civil rights in 88 BC.

Socrates (c. 470-399 BC) the most famous Athenian philosopher, his ideas were passed down primarily through the writings of Plato. He stressed virtue as knowledge, believing that if one knew the good, one would perform it rather than evil. Noted for his logic and style of questioning dialogue, he was condemned to death because of his alleged undermining of the democratic order.

Sophists itinerant teachers of philosophy, politics, and rhetoric in fifth-century Greece; noted for skill in clever but fallacious argument and persuasive rhetoric; provided instruction for a fee; most considered truth and morality relative; first to systematize education; notable Sophists were Hippias of Elis, Protagoras, Gorgias, and Prodicus of Ceos.

Sophocles (c. 496-406 BC) Greek tragic dramatist.

Sparta city-state in the southern Peloponnisos; isolated agricultural land power, resistant to external influences; oligarchy; fought Athens in the Peloponnesian War.

Stoicism Greek school of philosophy founded by Zeno (308 BC); considered all occurrences the result of logos or divine will; humans should be free of passion, emotion.

Sulla, Lucius Cornelius (Felix) (138-78 BC) Roman general and statesman; led the optimates (aristocratic party) during the civil war of 88-86 BC; praetor (93 BC); propraetor in Cilicia (92 BC); leader in the Social War (90-88 BC) against the northern Italian allies; consul (88 BC). In 83 BC, he defeated Marius's popular party, became dictator, instituted constitutional reform, restored senatorial power. He reorganized Rome's criminal procedures; resigned (79 BC).

Syracuse Corinthian colony on Sicily; flourished culturally and commercially in the fifth century BC and dominated the other Sicilian colonies. Syracuse resisted Athenian siege and defeated Athens with the help of Sparta (415-413 BC).

talent ancient unit of weight and money.

Tarentum major Greek colony in southern Italy. After a conflict with Thurii, which called for Roman aid, Tarentum hired Pyrrhus. He defeated the Romans in 280 and 279 BC. In 275 BC, Tarentum was again beleaguered. It surrendered in 272 BC.

Teutons a people who invaded southern France and Spain c. 111 BC; defeated by Marius in 102 and 101 BC.

Thebes Greek city-state; dominant under Epamenondas (371-362 BC); razed by Alexander the Great (335 BC).

Thirty Tyrants thirty oligarchs who ruled Athens (404-403 BC) following the Peloponnesian War; noted for their unrestricted use of power.

Thucydides (c. 460-c. 400 BC), early Greek historian; wrote *History of the Peloponnesian War* as it occurred.

tribune of the people Roman representative of the plebeians introduced in 494 BC to protect the lower class against the patricians and the senate, later represented all the people.

***tribus* (district)** division where Roman citizens were registered on the basis of landholdings and assessed taxes called *tributum*.

Varro, Gaius Terentius (?-c. 200 BC) consul with patrician Lucius Aemilius Paulus; favored an offensive against Hannibal.

Bibliography

The Greek City-States and
The Peloponnesian War
Connor, W. R. *Thucydides*. Princeton, 1987.
Ellis, W. *Alcibiades*. London, 1989.
Kagan, D. *The Outbreak of the Peloponnesian War*. Ithaca, 1969.
———. *The Archidamian War*. Ithaca, 1974.
———. *The Peace of Nicias and the Sicilian Expedition*. Ithaca, 1982.
Meiggs, R. *The Athenian Empire*. Oxford, 1972.

Greece after the Classical Period
Cartledge, P. *Agesilaos and the Crisis of Sparta*. London, 1987.
Ellis, J. R. *Philip II and Macedonian Imperialism*. London, 1976.
Hansen, M. H. *The Athenian Democracy in the Age of Demosthenes: Structure, Principles and Ideology*. Oxford, 1991.

Alexander the Great
Bosworth, A. B. *Conquest and Empire: The Reign of Alexander the Great*. Cambridge, 1988.
Engels, D. W. *Alexander the Great and the Logistics of the Macedonian Army*. Berkeley, 1978.
Lane Fox, R. *Alexander the Great*. London, 1973.
Tarn, W. W. *Alexander the Great*. Cambridge, 1948.

Hellenism
Bowman, A. K. *Egypt after the Pharaohs, 332 B.C.-A.D. 642*. Oxford, 1990.
Cary, M. *A History of the Greek World, 323 to 146 B.C.* London, 1951.
Ellis, W. M. *Ptolemy of Egypt*. London, 1993.
Fraser, P. H. *Ptolemaic Alexandria*. Oxford, 1972.
Green, P. *Alexander to Actium: The Historical Evolution of the Hellenistic Age*. Berkeley, 1993.
Heckel, W. *The Marshals of Alexander's Empire*. London, 1992.
Kincaid, C. A. *Successors of Alexander the Great*. Princeton, 1985.
Kuhrt, A., and Sherwin-White, S. *From Samarkand to Sardis: A New Approach to the Seleucid Empire*. Berkeley, 1993.

The Greek Legacy
Barker, E. *Greek Political Theory: Plato and His Predecessors*. London, 1918.
Farrington, B. *Greek Science*. Harmondsworth, 1961.
———. *The Faith of Epicurus*. New York, 1967.
Guthrie, W. K. C. *A History of Greek Philosophy*. Cambridge, 1962-1981.

Lesky, A. *A History of Greek Literature*. New York, 1966.
Long, A. A. *Hellenistic Philosophy: Stoics, Epicureans, Sceptics*. London, 1986.
Mohr, R. D. *Platonic Cosmology*. Leiden, 1985.
Neugebauer, O. *The Exact Sciences in Antiquity*. Princeton, 1952.
Pollitt, J. J. *Art in the Hellenistic Age*. Cambridge, 1990.
Taylor, A. E. *Plato: The Man and His Work*. London, 1926.

Ancient Rome
Alfoldi, A. *Early Rome and the Latins*. Ann Arbor, 1965.
Galinsky, G. K. *Aeneas, Siciliy, and Rome*. Princeton, 1969.
Gjerstadt, E. *Legends and Facts of Early Roman History*. Lund, 1962.
Grant, M. *Roman Myths*. London, 1971.

Patricians and Plebeians
Crawford, M. *The Roman Republic*, Fontana History of the Roman World. Glasgow, 1978.
Ferenczy, E. *From the Patrician State to the Patricio-plebeian State*. Amsterdam, 1976.
Ogilvie, R. M. *Early Rome and the Etruscans*, Fontana History of the Ancient World. Glasgow, 1976.
Raaflaub, K. A., ed. *Social Struggles in Archaic Rome: New Perspectives on the Conflict of the Orders*. Berkeley, 1986.

From City to State
Crawford, M. *The Roman Republic*, Fontana History of the Ancient World. Glasgow, 1978.
Harris, W. V. *Rome in Etruria and Umbria*. Oxford, 1971.
Keaveney, A. *Rome and the Unification of Italy*. London, 1987.
Pallottino, M. *Etruscologia*. Milan, 1975.
Salmon, E. T. *Samnium and the Samnites*. Cambridge, 1967.

Duel for the West
Bagnall, N. *The Punic Wars*. London, 1990.
Caven, B. *The Punic Wars*. London, 1980.
Conolly, P. *Hannibal and the Enemies of Rome*. London, 1978.
Errington, R. M. *The Dawn of Empire: Rome's Rise to World Power*. Ithaca, 1972.

The Roman Revolution
Astin, A. E. *Scipio Aemilianus*. Oxford, 1971.
Badian, E. *Foreign Clientelae*. Oxford, 1958.
Gruen, E. S. *The Hellenistic World and the Coming of Rome*, 2 vols. Berkeley, 1984.
Keaveney, A. *Sulla: The Last Republican*. London, 1982.
Stockton, D. *The Gracchi*. Oxford, 1979.

Further Reading

Abbott, Frank F. *The Common People of Ancient Rome.* Cheshire, CT, 1965.

Amery and Vanage. *Rome and Romans.* Tulsa, OK, 1976.

Bosworth, A.B. *Conquest and Empire: The Reign of Alexander the Great.* New York, 1993.

Church, Alfred J. *Roman Life in the Days of Cicero.* Cheshire, CT, 1978.

Cogan, Mark. *The Human Thing: The Speeches and Principles of Thucydides' History.* Chicago, 1981.

Connor, W. Robert. *Thucydides.* Princeton, 1987.

Davis, William S. *Day in Old Rome.* Cheshire, CT, 1963.

Fowler, Barbara H. *Hellenistic Aesthetic.* Madison, WI, 1989.

Ganeri, Anita. *Ancient Greece.* New York, 1992.

Green, Peter. *Alexander to Actium: The Historical Evolution of the Hellenistic Age.* Berkeley, 1993.

Hamilton, Charles D. *Sparta's Bitter Victories: Politics and Diplomacy in the Corinthian War.* Ithaca, 1978.

Harding, H. F. *The Speeches of Thucydides.* Lawrence, KS, 1973.

Hardy, W. G. *The Greek and Roman World.* Rochester, VT, 1970.

Henderson, Bernard W. *The Great War Between Athens and Sparta.* N. Stratford, NH, 1976.

Hodge, Peter. *Roman House.* White Plains, NY, 1971.

Kagan, Donald. *The Archidamian War.* Ithaca, 1974.

———.*The Fall of the Athenian Empire.* Ithaca, 1987.

———.*The Outbreak of the Peloponnesian War.* Ithaca, 1969.

Lamprey, Louise. *Children of Ancient Gaul.* Cheshire, CT, 1968.

———.*Children of Ancient Rome.* Cheshire, CT, 1967.

Nicholson, Robert. *Ancient Greece.* New York, 1992.

Orwin, Clifford. *The Humanity of Thucydides.* Princeton, 1994.

Plutarch. *The Age of Alexander.* Translated by Ian Scott-Kilvert. New York, 1973.

Sauvain, Philip. *Over Two Thousand Years Ago in Ancient Greece.* New York, 1992.

Savill, Agnes. *Alexander the Great.* New York, 1990.

Steele, Philip. *In Ancient Rome.* Morristown, NJ, 1995.

Toynbee, Arnold J. *Hellenism: The History of a Civilization.* Westport, CT, 1981.

Illustration Credits

AKG, Berlin, Germany 580-581, 625

British Museum, London/Bridgeman Art Library, London, England 593

E.T. Archive, London, England 598-599, 613

Ton van der Heyden, Naarden, The Netherlands 644, 659, 665, 689, 693

Musée de la Civilisation, Paris/Bridgeman Art Library, London, England 666

Musée Condé, Chantilly/Giraudon/ Bridgeman Art Library, London, England 607

Robert Harding Picture Library, London, England 631, 691

All other illustrations:
Salvat S.A., Barcelona, Spain and/or
HD Communication Consultants B.V., Hilversum, The Netherlands

Index

Text is indicated in roman type; illustrations are indicated in italic type.

715

Text is indicated in roman type; illustrations are indicated in italic type.

Text is indicated in roman type; illustrations are indicated in italic type.

717

Text is indicated in roman type; illustrations are indicated in italic type.

Text is indicated in roman type; illustrations are indicated in italic type.